VOLUME 18 · NUMBER 3 · FALL 2006

Studies in American Indian Literatures

EDITOR MALEA POWELL Michigan State University

Published by The University of Nebraska Press

SUBSCRIPTIONS

Studies in American Indian Literatures (*SAIL* ISSN 0730-3238) is the only scholarly journal in the United States that focuses exclusively on American Indian literatures. *SAIL* is published quarterly by the University of Nebraska Press for the Association for the Study of American Indian Literatures (ASAIL). Subscription rates are $30 for individuals and $75 for institutions. Single issues are available for $20. For subscriptions outside the United States, please add $20. Canadian subscribers please add 7% GST. To subscribe, please contact the University of Nebraska Press. Payment must accompany order. Make checks payable to the University of Nebraska Press and mail to:

Customer Service
1111 Lincoln Mall
Lincoln, NE 68588-0630
Telephone 800-755-1105 (United States and Canada)
402-472-3581 (other countries)
www.nebraskapress.unl.edu

All inquiries on subscription, change of address, advertising, and other business communications should be addressed to the University of Nebraska Press.

For information on membership in ASAIL or the membership subscription discount please contact:

Siobhan Senier
University of New Hampshire
Department of English
Hamilton Smith Hall
95 Main Street
Durham, NH 03824-3574

SUBMISSIONS

The editorial board of *SAIL* invites the submission of scholarly, critical, pedagogical, and theoretical manuscripts focused on all aspects of American Indian literatures as well as the submission of poetry and short fiction, bibliographical essays, review essays, and interviews. We define "literatures" broadly to include all written, spoken, and visual texts created by Native peoples.

Manuscripts should be prepared in accordance with the most recent edition of the *MLA Style Manual.* Please send three clean copies of the manuscript along with a self-addressed envelope and sufficient postage to permit the return of the reviewed submission, or you may submit by e-mail as an attachment (preferably in Rich Text Format [RTF]).

SAIL observes a "blind reading" policy, so please do not include an author name on the title, first page, or anywhere else in the article. Do include your contact information, such as address, phone number, and e-mail address, on a separate sheet with your submission. All submissions are read by outside reviewers. Submissions should be sent directly to:

Daniel Heath Justice
Department of English, University of Toronto
170 St. George Street
Toronto, ON M5B 2M8
Canada

Manufactured in the United States of America
SAIL is available online through Project MUSE at http://muse.jhu.edu.

Articles appearing in this journal are abstracted and indexed in Arts and *Humanities Citation Index®* and *Current Contents®/Arts & Humanities.*

Cover: Photo courtesy of Bonita Bent-Nelson © 2003, design by Kimberly Hermsen
Interior: Kimberly Hermsen

CONTENTS

Special Issue
Remembering James Welch

Volume 18, Number 3

GUEST EDITOR, KATHRYN W. SHANLEY

GUEST EDITOR'S PREFACE

Circling Back, Closing In

Remembering James Welch

KATHRYN W. SHANLEY
University of Montana

Introductions, like conclusions, draw time into a circle, moving clockwise or counterclockwise. Beginnings are revivified like the favorite old tunes we love to dance to again and again. Paying tribute to James Welch, for me, brings to mind dancing: James Welch as the poet/would-be fox dancer of his poem "Two for the Festival" (*Riding* 55). "Fox, the awkward dancer," is the descriptive phrase he uses for the younger persona in that poem. In pulling that metaphor from his work, I do not mean to romanticize Welch, for "dance" takes on deeply nuanced meanings in Native cultures, from social dance to Sun Dance, from celebration to sacrifice. Dance as a complex metaphor figures into the writing of poetry also. As James Tate writes in his introduction to *Riding the Earthboy 40*, poetry is "that magnificent dance of language that cannot be translated into prose" (viii). Jim Welch began as a poet, though he moved freely with and within many rhythms of language. When asked why he did not write poetry anymore, Jim often commented that he would like to believe poetry resides within his prose. I believe it does.

Paying tribute to James Welch concludes, yet oddly opens again, those fundamental questions about the meaning of life he posed in his poems. As Gail Tremblay's reading of his poem "Getting Things Straight" so tenderly shows, our questions shape our vision, and vice versa, what we are able to see, even when we do not necessarily understand it fully. Although clearly an extraordinary poet, Welch also had a great deal of the philosopher in him, one who sought another discourse, a different way of "explaining"—through narrative and humor—the ways, whys, and wherefores of Indian life and struggles.

He was a man of deep passion and commitment, who shunned easy sentiment. Thinking of him as tough-minded, kind-hearted, and doggedly determined to avoid easy solutions to or sloppy thinking about human dilemmas and sorrows, I remember Jim's invaluable contribution to Indian people. He has touched so many people's lives through his writing and his being, as the stories and essays that follow will tell.

How difficult his path was at times, and how cleverly he negotiated that path! In an interview in the 1970s, Jim talked about the "tyranny of expectations" he faced (Jahner 343).[1] He said,

> People expect you to do things a certain way, their way. Members of the arts councils think it's nice that a young Indian can express himself so eloquently on "the Indian experience." They secretly know that most Indians have trouble writing their names in mud with a sharp stick and are hence ineloquent, or uneloquent, noneloquent. And the young Indians you meet at colleges and high schools wonder why you are wearing a bow-tie and smiling so much at the people who are oppressing them and paying you to dance. (Loy 30)

Through his own self-deprecating humor, Jim expressed an understanding of the awkwardness of his position in the world as an Indian writer, and in doing so, he gave the rest of us courage.

He often talked about "getting it right" so that Indian people would recognize themselves and their realities in his writing, and again and again Indian people told him that he had indeed gotten it right. He had his detractors, as all of us do, but he attempted not to shrink from the brutal truths of cultural loss and sorrow. He always tried to look ahead, to read the magical hide of winter counts. He got something so right in *Winter in the Blood*, at least for me as an Indian reader in the early 1970s, that on a first read I experienced it as profoundly depressing. Its reality I knew in my heart and soul. The second time I laughed all the way through; that is how fundamentally Indian it seemed to me, capturing as it does life on the hi-line where I grew up, with its fragile hope and sometimes pathetic longing and despair yet doing so with a certain richness of human perspective.

I first met Jim in 1982 when, through a comical set of family circumstances, I was asked to give the keynote address at the Indian Council Fires annual awards banquet in Chicago. He was being honored with their American Indian Lifetime Achievement Award. The keynote speaker was usually a prominent Indian leader who talked about some contemporary issue in Indian Country. My sister, Dr. Lois Steele, then director of the Indians into Medicine Program at the University of North Dakota, was supposed to give the talk, but something came up at the last minute and she could not make it, so she suggested me. They were desperate, so desperate in fact that even a lowly graduate student who was just beginning a dissertation on the literary works of James Welch looked good to them.

Several things stand out in my memories about that night, including the crazy, eclectic talk I gave titled, in homage to his poem, "The Renegade Wants Words" (Welch, *Riding* 37). It was a talk that one attendee described to me afterward as more of a poetry reading than a speech. As I read poem after poem, Jim smiled in an encouraging way. The "renegades" in Zortman were hanged without "one good word" said about them, so I was determined to reiterate Welch's tribute to their resistance to European American encroachment and land-grabbing.[2] I remember reading a poem to the audience by Bertolt Brecht about capitalism and piling shit high. (It is embarrassing to think about it.)

With fondness, I recall how a core group of us—maybe a dozen or so—hung around to dance to the band after all the rest had gone home. We gathered in a circle, each taking a turn dancing in the center then pulling someone else in to take our place. Although Jim apologized for not being a dancer, he nonetheless stood around the circle like the rest of us with great appreciation of the fun being had by all.

Most significantly, I remember his gracious kindness toward me throughout the evening. I told a story in my talk about how, when I was a child, my grandmother taught me a good luck saying in Nakona and how it was Welch's work that helped me to understand "luck" in my grandmother's terms. It goes like this: When a nighthawk flies overhead, you are supposed to say, "Pishka, Pishka, me chesne na bo." My abundant, laughing grandmother would translate: "Nighthawk,

nighthawk, come shit on me, boy." Jim laughed and laughed when I said that. And at that moment he knew I knew something of what he meant, and I knew he knew something of the reservation life we both knew. It was a lot like the cosmic fart from the horse named Bird in *Winter in the Blood*—a humor that refuses sentimentality and takes luck where it can find it. Or was it just a fart?

Welch dared to call things as he saw them and in doing so opened a world of expression for other Native poets. He taught others about the possible by depicting those with little claim on possibility. He achieved that through a recognizably Indian grace. Although anyone who knew Jim personally would attest to his kind and gentle manner, his graciousness extended far beyond being a superficial habit of behavior. Joy Harjo in dedicating her prose poem "Grace" to Jim depicts the paradoxical and elusive nature of grace. She writes,

> I think of Wind and her wild ways the year we had nothing to lose and lost it anyway in the cursed country of the fox. We still talk about that winter, how the cold froze imaginary buffalo on the stuffed horizon of snowbanks. The haunting voices of the starved and mutilated broke fences, crashed our thermostat dreams, and we couldn't stand it one more time. So once again we lost a winter in stubborn memory, walked through cheap apartment walls, skated through fields of ghosts into a town that never wanted us, in the epic search for grace.
>
> . . . .
>
> . . . And one morning as the sun struggled to break ice, and our dreams had found us with coffee and pancakes in a truck stop along Highway 50, we found grace. (65)

One can imagine the greasy smell of bacon frying and the acrid pall of cigarette smoke hanging in the air yet also see this truck stop as a place of significance to these Indians in their own ritual moment. In concluding the poem, Harjo moves past the "dingy light" to a "promise of balance" and "the hope of children and corn" (65).

Listen closely to these lines from some of Jim's poems, and you will hear how Harjo echoes Welch: "I became / the statue needing friends in wind that needed fire, mountains to bang against" ("The Versatile Historian"); "To stay alive this way, it's hard" ("Surviving"); and "All around town, children ran out, / . . . / to create life, in their own image" ("The Day the Children Took Over"). Through his courage in daring to be himself, Jim taught us all something, and he told the truth as he saw it. He was a teacher whether he was standing in front of a class or giving advice to a specific individual.

Although he was not prone to offering a lot of advice, he (sort of) gave me advice three times: once he said he thought I should serve on the parole board. I think he wanted me to toughen up, see the whole historical process manifest in some rugged criminals. Once, through his wife, Lois, he told me I should not pick up hitchhikers; he had read too many criminal records to take chances with strangers. It had happened that on the way to their house I had picked up a hitchhiker who held up a sign saying, "I have a brain tumor. Need a ride to the grocery store." The man turned out to be pitiful and seemingly harmless, but I was glad when he got out of the car. I think both bits of advice from Jim came from the same brotherly place in him. The third piece of advice he gave me was to be a role model to other Indians, especially young people—it was a responsibility he took seriously, as the tributes in this issue by Ripley Hugo, Debra Magpie Earling, Neil McMahon, David Moore, and William Wetzel attest. He taught us all many valuable lessons without wagging a finger at us or touting his knowledge.

He had good teachers too. Richard Hugo, by Jim's own account, taught him to trust what he knew. "Two for the Festival" depicts that relationship so well—as whimsical and magical, though nonetheless serious. In Welch's comments dedicating the poem to Hugo, he writes, "I think the line 'Fox, the awkward dancer, hugged his stones' is Hugo. He combines Foxiness and awkwardness so well. I'm probably the young dancer trying to get some of those stones away from him" (Loy 37). When we read Hugo as the "usual customer," then, we are able to follow him in his clumsiness through a transformation from carrier of a blind toad, a fox, and thirteen lumpy stones to one who magically transforms the toad into a star in the heavens and who somehow incorporates the fox into his being and ardently clings to the thirteen lumpy stones for luck. He possesses paradoxical powers, lucky and unlucky, but his movement toward home is as sure as his need for one drink for the road. The young dancer surrealistically becomes confused with the young boy who drowns cats in clouds and gets his face blackened by playing with fire. The players touch and are touched by a magic as potentially harmful as it is beneficial.

Welch moved on from those poems, written in the late 1960s and early '70s, to rendering in his novels a view of human experience as real and magical at the same time, always circling back to the themes in the poems. And always a single-consciousness guides the poems and narratives, whether through a first- or a third-person narrator. Yet, it would be decidedly wrong to read Welch's works as though they mirror autobiographical events in this life. He was always careful to move beyond himself to a contemplative space where his reader could join him. Phillip Round's words speak well to the impetus behind many of Welch's works: "It is a lyric that meditates on a specific occasion and whose form models the speaker's transforming consciousness as he engages in contemplation." Welch's work, taken as a whole, is a meditation on what it means to be culturally Indian. As Roger Sale says of Welch's novel *Winter in the Blood*, there are "no vistas into the past, no invitation to nostalgia is ever made." From the narrator, "one may find out what it is like to be an Indian, this Indian, but just what that means is never offered for summary or conclusion" (20).

In his move from poetry to fiction, Welch did as creative writers are so often told to do: he wrote about what he knew of living in northeastern Montana (the Fort Belknap Reservation) and northwestern Montana (the Blackfeet Reservation). The questions that guide Welch's prose follow along the trajectory set in motion by his poetry, and those questions lead Welch's single-consciousness personae from Montana Hi-line anonymity and an internal monologue of sorts (*Winter in the Blood* and *The Death of Jim Loney*), through an historical and contemporary set of circumstances (*Fools Crow* and *The Indian Lawyer*), and eventually to cultural invisibility and voicelessness in the France of *The Heartsong of Charging Elk*. The stop he makes along the way to write *Killing Custer* functions as an authorial aside in the author's musings. Welch's existential questions, however, are never laid to rest; from the first to the fifth novel, he ponders Indianness by way of pondering being, or vice versa, not seeking to escape being Indian, but rather to grasp its meaning. Being Indian is his lot.

As William Bevis notes, "Welch's first two novels pose the same question: Has the hero/narrator improved his lot? Is there any redemption or success in this Highline world of poverty, distance and booze?" (118). By way of "answering" those questions, the poetic stills in these narratives of circling movement create "anti-narrative" moments, particularly in *Winter in the Blood*, that beg us "not to read on but to stop and think about what we have just read," as Bevis also notes, "forcing us to search for connections among the shards" (119). In that way, readers enter the world they would otherwise drive by on Highway 2 as tourists; they are forced to see the humanity in the characters, the old in the new.

The nameless narrator of *Winter* might be seen in his staggering movement from one bar to the next and perhaps even be viewed with disgust as "the drunken Indian," but once readers have seen from the inside out, as it were, that world can never be quite the same. All protagonists in Welch's novels, as isolated and isolative as they may be most of the time, exist within a matrix of relations, both human and of other species. The women especially complete the whole; as Patrice Hollrah notes, "The women's emotions are needed to comment on what happens," an observation taken from the beginning of *Charging Elk*, where the men face defeat. It is almost as if the self or protagonist in each work is looking out into the world mutely, unable to express his pain in a way that would be visible to others.

With *The Death of Jim Loney*, Welch shifts the point of view to that of a could-have-been hero, albeit on a small scale, who ponders his life and fate consciously. Epochs of history circumscribe the narrator's life, as he faces decisions about whether or not to leave the reservation. He somehow gets caught between dark and dawn, between the Judeo-Christian dispensations of Law and of Grace, between historical doom and regenerative possibility. As if an answer to the ideological implications of American Manifest Destiny, the plot unfolds between Thanksgiving and Christmas, and the protagonist dies in a sense before he is born, on Christmas Eve. But rather than die "killed beyond recognition," Loney makes a public spectacle of dying. In the novel, "killed beyond recognition" is from the back-page newsline of a third-rate newspaper, describing and reporting the death of Loney's friend Yellow Eyes. Yellow Eyes had been run over by a train somewhere between Bozeman and Butte, Montana. Metaphorically, "killed beyond recognition" represents a silence and a silencing; no one ever asks what happened to Yellow Eyes. The one time Loney shares the "news" with Pretty Weasel he thinks to himself, I "felt almost human" (115). Jennifer Lemberg takes the position that "to say that Loney's death, or his life, is devoid of Indian features is to discount the losses he suffers. In fact, *The Death of Jim Loney* offers a compelling portrait of one man's culturally specific response to a history of trauma." The details of that history, shards, we must intuit for ourselves.

With *Fools Crow*, Welch takes readers back into the Pikuni history that allows insight into the defeatedness of other Welchian protagonists and personae. For Montana Indian peoples "the history of trauma" means nineteenth-century small pox epidemics, white encroachment upon their lands, multiple treaties resulting in a shrinking homeland, the breaking up of families through allotment of land, starvation, alcohol abuse, and despair. *Fools Crow*, as Welch himself says, provides "a much larger landscape than the other two novels, and it shows where some of the younger characters in the first two books are coming from" (qtd. in McFarland 109).The symbolic depiction of the novel's characters, as Bette Weidman asserts, "frames their activity on the timeless space of ritual," through a device of the procession, which has "a long history in religion and in American literature." Constructing as he does the stage to dramatize that moment in Plains Indian history allows Welch to complete a sort of exorcism of historical trauma and grief in preparation for his next books, which move into portrayals of success.

With both *The Indian Lawyer* (1990) and *Killing Custer* (1994), Welch shifts toward less defeated moments in the lives of historical and fictional Indian people. Although *The Indian Lawyer* was written first, *Killing Custer* links more readily with *Fools Crow*, even as it anticipates *The Heartsong of Charging Elk*. The defeat of Custer had begun to be seen differently by the country after the turmoil of the 1970s, especially with the renaming of the national park site the Little Big

Horn Battlefield. Of the site, Welch explains that "Indians come from all over America" to experience the place, "because this site represents a moment of glory for Indian people, and they can stand on hallowed ground walked on and ridden over by some of the most noble 'hostiles' ever assembled in Indian country" (*Killing Custer* 103). He is reclaiming Indian Country and foregrounding Indian pride.

The Indian Lawyer unpredictably takes up a middle-class, professional Indian. Instead of writing about the down-and-outers he came to know through his work on the parole board or those unjustly accused and incarcerated (and they do exist), Welch chose to shape his next protagonist into a contender for the U.S. Senate. Quite fittingly, Sylvester Yellow Calf himself knows the basketball success of a Jim Loney, and yet he brokers the support and success with which he was blessed into an education and a good life, upward social mobility. Nonetheless, his own failings bring him to an assessment of his life and a commitment to Indian people. In a way, Sylvester bears a resemblance to Welch's three previous protagonists: the bungling character in *Winter*, the deadly serious Loney, and the heroic Fools Crow.

Perhaps at the moment when the wolves no longer howl at the door and when a person's conscious choice to belong drives him to live and care for others, a new sort of fragility emerges. Welch's move from a character such as Sylvester to one such as Charging Elk represents a pragmatism that grows out of a bedrock of centeredness. Andrea Opitz refers to the newborn state of Charging Elk as precarious indeed: "Left behind like a ghost in this highly ambiguous space, Charging Elk exposes how the 'Indian' is repeatedly produced as vanishing, quite literally, at the end of the show." Circling back on himself, Welch brings that single consciousness to indeterminacy once again, and since his books seem to pair off to explore facets of "The Indian's" existential dilemma, we can only wonder what his next novel would have posed. He was going to return Charging Elk to America, I have heard. We can only imagine the next pattern in his web of relatedness!

Circling back to his poems: one of my favorite moments in Welch's work comes from "Snow Weavers," a quiet poem about making meaning through words. Hope delicately and tentatively abides in the fact that "Wolves are dying at my door, / the winter drives them from their meat," and the narrator comments to the friend or lover who is listening, "Say this: say in *my* mind / I saw *your* spiders weaving threads to bandage up the day" (emphasis added). The dream leap between *my* and *your*, a magnificent dance of minds, tumbles wind into meaning and "meaning into wind" (*Riding* 43). Following Welch's trail, we can sense the wolves behind him, even at his door, but know of his narrow escape. We will miss him, and we will always wonder where he would have led us next.

NOTES

Contributions to the James P. Welch Memorial Scholarship Fund, a scholarship that will support a Native American student in English, will be welcomed by the University of Montana Foundation, c/o Julia Horn, Brantley Hall East Wing, Missoula, MT 59812.

1. Christine Cald McGonigle uses the phrase "tyranny of expectations" to describe the difficulties A. B. Guthrie Jr., James Welch, and Richard Hugo face as western writers (1).

2. The Zortman-Landusky Mine, land the Fort Belknap Assiniboines and Gros Ventres were forced to sell, was the

> largest leach gold mine in production in the Western world. . . . [In the early 1980s] the gross value of the gold and silver taken from the mines ranged between $20 to 25 million . . . when the entire reservation [was generating] only $100,000 in annual income. (Bryan 36)

When Pegasus Gold Mining Company went bankrupt in 1998, they left behind contamination of the land surface as well as the groundwater. For more details regarding Indigenous peoples and mining, see No Dirty Gold, "Toll on Indigenous Peoples," http://www.nodirtygold.org/toll_on_indigenous_peoples.cfm.

WORKS CITED

Bevis, William W. "Welch's Winters and Bloods." *Ten Tough Trips: Montana Writers and the West.* Norman: U of Oklahoma P, 1990. 117–39.

Bryan, William, Jr. "The Great Gold Robbery." *Montana Indians: Yesterday and Today.* 2nd ed. Helena: American and World Geographic Publishing, 1996. 38

Harjo, Joy. "Grace." *How We Became Human: New and Selected Poems: 1975–2001.* New York: W. W. Norton, 2004. 65.

Jahner, Elaine. "Introduction: American Indian Writers and the Tyranny of Expectations." *Book Forum* 5:3. Special Issue. Ed. Elaine Jahner. Rhinecliff, NY: Hudson River P, 1981. 343–48.

Loy, Dana. "James Welch: Finding His Own Voice." *Four Winds*. Austin, TX: Hundred Arrows P, 1980. 35–39.

McFarland, Ron, ed. *Understanding James Welch*. Columbia: U of South Carolina P, 2000.

McGonigle, Christine Cald. "Tyranny of Expectations: The Western Myth in the Work of Three Montana Writers." PhD diss., University of Washington, 1982.

Sale, Roger. "Winter's Tale." *New York Review of Books*, December 12, 1974, 20.

Tate, James. Introduction. *Riding the Earthboy* 40. By James Welch. New York: Penguin, 2004. vii–viii.

Welch, James. *The Death of Jim Loney*. New York: Harper and Row, 1979.

———. *Riding the Earthboy* 40. 1971. Reprint, New York: Penguin, 2004.

Welch, James, with Paul Stekler. *Killing Custer*. New York: W. W. Norton, 1994.

The Pleasure of His Company

LOIS M. WELCH
University of Montana

The smile, the smile. Eighty-five percent of the letters of condolence I received mentioned Jim's smile as their fondest memory of him. For a foolish moment I considered planning a segment of his memorial service about that smile. That is the Jim I want to remember here: the smiling, generous, surprising Jim.

As Jim's wife, I leave the bronze plaque stuff to others. What I loved about him was the fun. The fun was what made me love him. What I want to try to convey is the quality of the pleasure it was to be with him. He had the broadest and most nuanced emotional range of anyone I have known. His easy responsive laughter. His unflinching look at tragedy. The attentive intimacy of his gaze. His curiosity. His pleasure in the world around him—verbal, sensual, intellectual pleasure. His willingness to do the spontaneous. His potential goofiness. (He insisted, for instance, on a trip through Sun Valley that I take a snapshot of him alongside Hemingway's grave, *lying* beside the grave.) He was even a genial drunk. Never malicious, never carping or contemptuous. (Sometimes cranky.) He was more fun to be with than anyone I have known. He liked artichokes the first time I served him one—how could one not love him? This is not to say he was fun all the time; we all lapse into humdrum routines (though I suspect writers thrive on routine). Of course, he had his moods, annoyances, and flaws. Of some people one speaks tolerantly of balance between the good qualities and the bad. In Jim's case, I know of no one who disliked him. Here I want to sketch a few of these delights, since a definitive portrait is impossible in these few pages.

First of all, living with Jim was fun. Living with a writer is a bit like your childhood expectations of a refrigerator come to life. The light really *is* still on when the door is shut. Something is going on inside the refrigerator, and you will never quite figure out what. (In real life, what goes in comes back out in about the same shape.) Writers tend to obsess; they tend never to stop thinking about their current project, no matter what they are doing. One must accept this. With painters, you can see bit by bit what they are painting; with a writer, it may be a long time before you are shown any pages. Lest romantics get excited, we did not sit by the fire and read to each other of an evening. Jim only showed me what he was working on when he was nearly finished with a draft or when he wanted specific feedback. When I first knew him, he was writing poems, so of course I got to read new poems almost every day for a couple of years. That was an amazing period. I would come home from school, he would show me "Magic Fox" or some such new poem, we would go for a walk, fix dinner. Little did I know we were living the Native American Literary Renaissance. Later, there were long stretches, when he was writing the novels, when the fridge remained closed, as it were. But what surprises when it opened! He acted as though it were perfectly ordinary, and it was—his pleasantly lit study, his typewriter (then his computer), the same baseball cards on the wall then as now. He would hand me some chapters from, say, *Fools Crow*, and I would read them. I was always surprised, sometimes amazed.

Trailing in Jim's wake was fun too. I shall follow Jim's example and not drop names, but what a lot of writers and Native American scholars he got to know, and I beside him. Most of our friends were writers. The literary events and the travel were bonuses. Jim was enormously popular in France, and he loved it: he established close friendships with his editor and translator and others. It helped that I speak French. We never got enough of exploring both Paris and the countryside, where French history and culture are still visible.

From a certain angle, Jim was sublimely ordinary. He liked to watch sports on TV; he admitted to liking macaroni and cheese, and hamburgers. His impulse was always to blend in, not to stand out. His dress code was to be as unobtrusive as possible: crisp button-down shirts, twill trousers, no fringes, no neckties unless absolutely required (a reception with French President Chirac, for instance, was not for him an occasion requiring a tie), no t-shirts with messages, no feathers (*especially* no feathers), no jewelry. Inside this ordinary world, life could be remarkably sharp and interesting.

Jim saw with extraordinary intensity, noticing and remembering details of places with an almost painterly eye. (The Hopi painter Dan Lomahaftewa said he decided to become a painter after reading *Winter in the Blood.*) To some degree I attribute this visual acuity to his having gotten glasses only when he was in seventh grade: in grade school he had concluded that the smart kids were the ones who could read what was on the blackboard; he had to come up and sharpen his pencil to do so. That intense effort to see what was around him had surely become habitual by the time glasses made it easier. So just being with Jim was to inhabit one's surroundings more vividly. He saw antelope and deer, rabbits and bird nests where the rest of us see brown blurs.

Jim could be surprising. Not whimsical or unpredictable, simply surprising. One glistening Thanksgiving weekend, not long after we married, after having visited Jim's parents in north-central Montana, we were driving west and home. At that point in our lives, Jim was still teaching me to *see* the plains. (I was still part of that heartless tribe who equate mountains with scenery, considering the plains empty, desolate.) As we drove along, Jim was telling me about hunting pheasant, antelope, and deer in that Milk River country, about how he and his brother liked to track animals. My father was a marine biologist, so I had often combed the seashore with my siblings but had never gone hunting. Jim suddenly pulled over, led me out onto the thin crusty snow, and said, "Let's find some tracks." Crunching slowly through the two or three inches of snow, we gazed intently at the crust over the frozen wheat. Soon he came upon tiny little tracks: mouse tracks. Mouse tracks! We followed mouse tracks from one tiny burrow to another. One set of tracks merely stopped in mid-trail—lunchtime for hawks, he suspected.

One never knew what would turn up. Once he brought back from some trip, wrapped in his handkerchief, a perfect little mouse skull he had found. More often he would bring me back a pretty little rock, if a reading tour had left him an outdoor moment. (He always carried a pocket rock himself, a kind of talisman.) He would find hummingbird nests, bits of fur, and feathers. One sunny Sunday afternoon during the year in Greece when he wrote *Winter in the Blood*, we picked a bunch of wild flowers on a hill above the sea; the rule was no blossoms bigger than your little fingernail.

Jim was also surprising intellectually. Having been a mediocre student, disliking school, he disparaged his own intelligence and was impatient of theoretical abstractions. Much of that was self-protective, I decided, a way to resist appropriation—by teachers, critics, anthropologists. That he always wrote clear copy should have been a clue: no misspellings, very few revisions. His comments on writing were often breathtakingly astute. ("Your story starts here," he would say "on page 5," and it did.) While it is not my place to assess his writing (that is for the bronze plaque folks), it always struck me as both smart and wise.

From the get-go, we seemed to share a sense of humor, laughing at the same things. Jim was not given to telling jokes but had a delicious comic sense. In the fall of 1973, the *AWP Chronicle* asked him for an author photo to accompany some poems for a special Indian poetry section. Not yet having a formal author photo, Jim sent a snapshot I had taken of him, wearing cutoffs, in midstream, holding up in triumph a six-inch fish. The macho poet. My thirty-six-year tutorial in Native American history, culture, and humor was one of the bonuses of our marriage.[1]

I knew I had crossed a cultural divide when in 1975 Jim was reading one of the bar scenes in his first novel, *Winter in the Blood*, at the University of Arizona. I noticed that out of the fifty mainly white people in the audience, I was the only person laughing. Afterward Jim suggested that non-Indians did not know yet that Indians could be funny; they were still under the influence of Curtis photos and Westerns, so they expected high cheek bones, feathers, and a stoic demeanor.[2] They did not feel authorized to laugh. It did not seem to bother him.

My tutorial consisted mainly of learning context, finding the hilarious entwined with the hair-raising, watching outrage vanquished by the outrageous. Jim got to say "Rez Car"; I did not. He said "Enit Raymond?" at the end of a lot of sentences, and it took me a while to recognize that "enit" means "isn't it" and that Raymond was his generic Indian. Jim laughed harder at dog-eating Sioux jokes than I was allowed to. (For example, "What's a Sioux picnic? A beer and a six pack of puppies." A Navajo joke.) He loved calling himself a "Pelle Rosso," Italian for "redskin," a phrase he learned from a Neapolitan campground owner. He loved Indian teasing and joking. He did not like being called "Chief," even in jest, something only non-Indians seemed to do.

I cherish still a memento of my tutorial. Sometime in the 1970s, Jim and I were walking out on the Fort Belknap Reservation in north-central Montana, where his parents lived, and came across an old 1954 Hudson WASP rusting beside a road. He pried off its shiny chrome hood ornament—inscribed "WASP"—shined it on his sleeve, and formally held it out to me. "Welcome," he said, "from my people to your people."[3]

Jim had explained patiently how "his people" did not lecture, explain, analyze, or theorize. I grew up in academe and could barely imagine such a state of affairs. To prepare me to visit his parents, he described their conversational rhythm: Someone tells a story. Punch line ends the story. Laughter, perhaps. Pause. Someone says "Yep." Long pause. Someone else chimes in, "Yep, good old Smith [or whoever]." Pause. Then someone starts a new story. No interrupting. No mini-lectures. Thus prepared, we visited. They chatted. I listened. It wasn't long before someone said "Yep" after an anecdote and its pause. I choked down a guffaw. Some of those pauses were very long. Ever after, at home, when one of us would tell a story, and there seemed nothing to add, no response required, we would *simultaneously* intone, after a pause, "Yep," and the nonteller would add, "She won't be long now." Eventually, "Yep" after a long silence became its own punch line for us.

Everyone talks about Jim's sense of humor; they write about his irony, his satire, his black humor. He never explained, just deflected the conversation to Indian humor.[4] How he laughed! He even had what I called the "Tate giggle"—whenever his friend the poet James Tate called, I would know, not from any words, but from the giggles that constituted the majority of their phone calls. Jim loved having fooled his French editor into believing that the maximum security prison in *Heartsong of Charging Elk* actually existed. Richard Hugo—Jim's teacher, my colleague, our friend and neighbor—was a consummate storyteller. Jim assimilated many Hugo stories and punch lines. (For example, "And I could hold the chickens.") They talked often about timing in comedy and poetry. Jim's timing on and off the page was expert, sophisticated. When I first knew him, Jim was fairly shy, and though he gradually learned to operate in the public eye, he never wanted to hog the limelight. He surprised even his friends with the hilarious anecdotes he sandwiched, straight faced, between poems even at his earliest readings (see, for example, the interview in the Spring 1971 issue of *Jeopardy*). Admittedly, there was less and less psychic space for humor in his novels, but that did not affect his sense of humor in real life. Since he could be so deadpan, I rather pitied the poor editor who nagged Jim for his Indian name. (He did not have one.) Jim told me one night he was just going to tell the guy his Indian name was Types-at-Night. The nagging stopped; the name was never printed, of course, though his friends frequently called him Types-at-Night after he told the story.

Name changes often stuck: after a Chicano writer called Joy Harjo "Yoy" at a some conference they all attended, Jim called her "Yoy" forever after. Along with many of our friends, we came to call the nearby Nine Pipe Wildlife Refuge on the Flathead Reservation "Neenay Peepay" in memory of the unfortunate visiting eastern journalist who gushed on about how beautiful "Neenay Peepay" was, obviously feeling as foreign here as in central Africa. Often on a Sunday we would say, "Let's go to Neenay Peepay."[5]

Though ubiquitous, Native American humor, and Jim's in particular, was not malicious even when satirical. In Indian Country, a sense of humor is required, a survival tool in the face of ancient and continuing adversity. Jim did not tell me this, but I learned it quickly—from him, from his books, from his Indian friends.

Most tellingly, I learned from a startling discussion of the difference between Euramerican and Indian sacred play the Euramerican anticomic bias.[6] In Indian Country the clown is no minor mystic, no mere counterbalance to authority; he participates fully in a glorious divine vision of transformation and kinship. We Euramericans do not *get* this, culturally speaking. Joseph Epes Brown, the scholar of Native American studies, got it and says, "[Black Elk] understood that there is no access to a deeper spiritual reality if there is not the opening force of laughter present. It tends to open the heart for receiving greater values than those of this world."[7] That "opening force of laughter" is wonderful. Opening the heart—through laughter—for receiving greater values. Such unruliness is not merely disruptive, as postmodernist theory would have us believe; it opens a space in which imaginative reach and cognitive power can flourish once again.

Jim often lived in such a space, I believe, a space into which laughter freed him, where he felt both entirely free and entirely connected with the world around him. There was great acceptance rather than evasion of reality in his smile, in his laughter. (Drunkenness often puts one in an equivalent mood, but one's powers are limited.) He showed how that sense of connection leads directly to courage, while the sense of freedom triggers the imaginative reach and cognitive power that manifests itself creatively. Jim seemed to have available to him at any given moment the full range of his past life and learning. I have seen other writers pop out with poems memorized years before. As a linear thinker myself, I was surprised and grateful for his "outside-the-box" eruptions into my life—from his unexpected suggestions for dinner to off-the-wall quotes from *Leave it to Beaver* or Auden.

Jim's deep sense of connection to his world gave him at once his profound sense of humor, his courage, and his honesty, I now believe. He was honest rather than sentimental. He had the best BS detector I ever knew. He could detect the faintest whiff of inflated ego or smugness as clearly as he could measure the aptness of a particular word. Though raised a practicing Catholic, he distrusted all spiritual talk and New Age hooha (as he called it). He found his own ways to convey his bountiful vision of the world. Writing this now, at his desk, I face his photo of Chief Mountain (sacred to the Blackfeet), two bronze bears, some feathers, and a coffee mug whose handle is a naked blond woman—the sacred and the profane here together, unabashed. Beyond, the totem pole in the yard, the wooden bear nearly engulfed in shrubs.

Jim made no sentimental gestures—ignoring family birthdays, for example. Sentimentality pretends to feeling and to unfelt reverence. One morning, long before dawn, Jim was showering, prefatory to taking a seven o'clock flight. I was getting the coffee going. Not quite believing my ears, I heard chanting: Jim was requesting a bath towel as though he were intoning mass. Here in his study, he hung the All You Can Eat Chinese Buffet Gilroy calendar with its picture of the Arc de Triomphe, enjoying the conjunction of contradictory cultures. He plonked a big feather in the arms of one little bronze bear, obscuring its face, as though it were a huge sacred burden. It pleased him.

People think of Jim and often think kind and gentle, honest and unsentimental. Let's think courageous for a moment. It takes a certain courage to find amusing the sorts of things that are secretly freighted with meaning in our culture: Mothers' Day cards, for example. We must not lose sight of Jim's intercultural status: required sentimental gestures in white culture seem merely silly to those outside. The kind of courage I am thinking of is behavior that stems from a feeling of interconnectedness with one's surroundings.[8] Jim approached people, critters and things—everywhere—with a kind of parity. He was a genuine egalitarian. He did not like skunks, for example, but he did not want to shoot them. He did not like Republicans, but he did not waste time raging at them.[9] That does not mean he had saintly patience: many an offensive book about Custer and the Indians was hurled across his study before he completed *Killing Custer*.

Because he was a Montana guy, I suppose I expected Jim to be tough, a bit macho. Macho he was not; he had considerable reserves of strength and toughness. I came to understand the courage of the shy. Oddly, driving was where I first noticed the courage. He knew exactly what a car could do on an icy mountain pass—when he could pass a truck, when he must or we would lose our traction. I would be white-knuckled. He was merely all business—all competence, attention, courage.

It was courageous of him to confront a large drunken friend making a scene at some party, terrifying everyone. Jim got up, walked over, and told him in a quiet, firm voice to go outside until he could control himself. The friend did, and did. Jim still felt connected with the friend. The rest of us disconnected with what we suddenly saw as a monster.

It was courageous of him speak to Norman Mailer in a New York elevator on the way up to a literary party, saying he too was a writer and how much he admired Mailer's work. He got the cold shoulder—a slight glance, a mumble, no handshake. That experience left him more nervous about introducing himself years later to another much-admired writer, Joseph Heller; Heller, however, welcomed Jim, and they had a gratifying conversation.

In a larger sense, I believe now that it was courageous of Jim to go to university, or at least to continue his university education after flunking out of two schools. His family had moved around a lot; he had lived on and off reservations, going to high school in Minneapolis. He was used to adjusting to different places. His parents encouraged him, though neither had gone to college (his older brother had done well in college and went on to be a forester). There were just sixteen Native American students at the University of Montana in 1964; they got together in the Indian Club. Jim always downplayed any potential praise for finishing university when so many Indians did not, saying he was "just at loose ends."[10] In the same self-deprecating vein, he told one anthologist that he became a poet because he could not "make model airplanes like Lester Lame Deer or throw a calf like Albert Heavy Runner." When I told him that was witty, he replied that it was simply true.

And truly, I do not think becoming a writer was a huge step when Jim took it. It was just the next step. (He was not set on becoming a Great American Writer, just a poet like the other poets he knew.) He had always liked reading and had been writing poems, and then he was suddenly writing good poems, and then he was getting published, and then we were getting married and he could keep on writing, and he did. And then he wrote a novel, then rewrote the novel, and then his editor liked it, and so on. He did have some dark moments, as when the reviews were bad, but sometimes rejection seemed to inspire an anger-driven resolve. (He was not fun in those moods.) Of course, he was delighted at positive reviews, royalty checks, prizes, and his personal morsel of fame. In my diary in November 1974, I noted how we "giggled until we fell asleep" after his editor called to say *Winter in the Blood* was to be reviewed on the front page of the *New York Times Book Review*.[11]

Most important, Jim's sense of the interconnectedness of things gave him the courage to explore ever more deeply the Indian world that was his subject matter. If one's heart is open to it all, and all of it is connected, then the horror of massacres, the violence of hunting, and the hardship of winters and work coexist on the same spectrum as feasts and foolishness. Whenever asked, Jim always said writing was a process of discovery, and one can almost draw an arc of increasing profundity as he explored the lives of his various characters—often past the point of despair. It is tantalizing in retrospect to remember how he loved Homer, Milton, and Spenser in college; a tilt from lyric toward epic seems discernible to me in his writing. Of course, Hemingway, Faulkner, Vittorini, Vallejo, Bly, Wright, Ritsos, and Hugo were his favorite writers always.

Clearly, this sense of connection to the world was Jim's from his childhood. I learned this from Jim's mother, who was no big reader of poetry but called to thank Jim for her copy of *Riding the Earthboy 40* in the summer of 1971. He was off on a reading tour, so I got to hear from her one of the finest reviews he ever got: "He was the quiet one," she said, "but I knew he was the one paying attention. He knew the way things used to be and how they never will be again."

I want to air a theory. Jim's poems always seemed to me to be—linguistically—unlike those of any other poet. In part, I attribute this to a very early bilingualism. When he was small, his grandmother lived with the family, so they talked Blackfeet at home. Jim often went, as a small boy, with his father to talk with the old men who sat on the bench in front of Sherburne's Mercantile in Browning. They all talked in Blackfeet. Though he no longer remembered any Blackfeet when I knew him, I still believe that his early immersion in the language affected his psyche and his language.[12] In this view, *Fools Crow* would be a natural extension of that "Native textuality" by which he reclaims both his country and its lost culture. (See Andrea Opitz, this issue.)

It does not even sound like courage when I say Jim seemed always ready for the next step, ready for the demands of that next step, whatever it was. Yet he disliked complications. Avoided hassle. Appearing masterful was not one of his tricks. Among complications he disliked were lists of phone calls, letters to answer, assembling objects purchased in cartons, keeping expense accounts. Even if courage comes from feeling connected to one's environment, connecting to fifty kinds of nuts and bolts would still be daunting. He called for help. No Luddite, however, he loved roaring around on his riding mower.

On the other hand, agreeing to serve on the Montana Board of Pardons was a step for which he was not sure he was prepared. If it took courage, it also inspired trepidation. The dean of the law school had goaded him to accept the appointment by reminding him that 30 percent of prison inmates were Indian, and if Jim—an intelligent and good-hearted Indian—did not accept, some redneck rancher from eastern Montana would. Ten years he served on the board, attending monthly sessions at the prison, reading voluminous reports on each prospective parolee. It was emotionally exhausting. It toughened him in a certain way. He became more outspoken and pragmatic: "Okay," he would tell a prisoner, "I agree; you've had a terrible life so far. Now what do you want? Maybe we can help you attain that." He once got so irritated at a self-pitying rancher/prisoner that he coldly read aloud each of the twelve counts on which the guy had been convicted and then asked him what precisely he felt innocent *of*. Though most of us like to think criminals are quite different sorts of people from us, Jim felt increasingly that the line between those who were in prison and those who were out was fuzzy and rather accidental. Again, that sense of connectedness, that parity among creatures. (By the way, very little of that experience could be called fun, but both of us gained a whole new perspective from those years.)

Of course, the most courageous act of his life was living out his last year with lung cancer. One day he said he would like to see—just once—an obituary that said so-and-so had died after a long and *cowardly* battle with cancer. During that whole year, Jim was never angry, never in denial, never self-pitying. He always greeted the question "How are you?" with a smile and an upbeat "fine"—even on the day he died. Of course, he often felt lousy, got grumpy. But he looked straight at it, the way he had most problems in his life. Toward the end of his illness, he said he would much rather have a party with all his friends right now than a big old memorial service when he would not be around to enjoy it. He had not, alas, the energy for it. But the morning of the day he died, a dear friend came by with a giant bouquet of flowers fresh from her garden; by chance, another friend, two neighbors, three dogs, and a child followed her into the house, turning it into a kind of procession—a cheerful commotion indeed. He loved it. He smiled and smiled.

NOTES

1. In the interests of full disclosure, we married June 22, 1968, having met at an opening day of fishing season party in May the previous year. I came to the University of Montana in the fall of 1966 as an assistant professor of English to teach literary criticism and drama. Jim had received his bachelor's degree in 1965 and had begun graduate work in creative writing that fall.

2. I will use the term "Indian" for Indigenous people because they do.

3. He used the term "my people" only ironically, knowing its hyper-generalization.

4. I was the one who taught courses in comedy; my job was to theorize.

5. Family nicknames were surprisingly bold, hilarious—and omitted here to protect the innocent and/or guilty.

6. See Kenneth Lincoln's *Indi'n Humor: Bicultural Play in Native America* (Oxford UP, 1993).

7. Lincoln, *Indi'n Humor*, 67.

8. I exclude the kind of courage, if it can be called that, that must climb mountains "because they are there," the kind that basks in challenges and sings praises of its own derring-do.

9. In truth, he did listen to Paul Harvey over lunch every day, just to "get his juices jangling," as he called it, to remind himself how bigotry parades as righteousness and other such annoyances.

10. We should not forget that, like most students, Jim was avoiding the draft during the Sixties.

11. By contrast, his biggest award came about in a stunningly mundane manner. In August of 1995 Jim was mowing the lawn when the FedEx truck came by, so I took and opened the big envelope that contained a letter and a certificate stating that Jim had been made a "Chevalier de l'ordre des arts et des lettres" by the Ministre de culture et de la Francophonie of the French

government. We were mystified but only learned that it was the real thing, and a Big Deal, when we faxed it to his French editor—who was thrilled. Then Jim was.

12. It probably also needs to be said that Jim found learning foreign languages quite difficult. He managed, rather hilariously, I thought, to make appropriate Spanish, Italian, Greek, and French noises for moving in society but would never settle down to study vocabulary. Like a good poet, he loved the sounds, the rhythms of languages, but let me conduct the verbal business.

A Generous Friend

RIPLEY HUGO

James and Lois Welch were fast friends of Richard Hugo. When I married Dick, they welcomed my children and me into that friendship. We were neighbors on the same street too. Over the years my children ran down to Jim and Lois with their problems. Lois taught Melissa about sewing; Jim wrote Matt a recommendation for college. One Christmas season, Jim went with them to bring back a tree for each of our houses. Lois and Jim became our extended family, and after Dick's death in 1982, they helped me edit Dick's essays.

I remember how calmly Jim insisted that I could learn to use a computer when I was sure I could not. He took the time to bring me his used computer, set it up, and then painstakingly show me how to work it. I had to measure up because he was not a friend I wanted to disappoint.

I remember too a summer night out in our backyard under the poplar trees. A bunch of us were sitting on benches around the picnic table after supper, drinking beer and talking. Jim was across the table from me, talking with Melissa and her latest boyfriend. Some moments they were both talking to Jim at once, all three faces shining in the candlelight. Jim often nodded, listened in his intent way, and made some pithy comment. Suddenly, the young man called Jim "Governor," and the name stuck. Whenever in the years to come Melissa addressed Jim as "Governor," he accepted with a slight smile, as if he considered the honor his due.

* * *

In 1983 when Matt, only twenty-two, was hospitalized in Seattle,

Washington, for cancer treatments, he looked out the window at the steady rain one day and said suddenly, "Mom, I haven't done shit." I wanted to cry out "No!" Instead, I told him he had, that he had written good poems, that maybe he could use this time to revise them and put them together as a manuscript. He seized the idea. I brought his poems to him from our home in Montana. Every day that he could, he worked on the poems and completed his manuscript. When he thought it was good enough, he said shyly that he would send it to Jim to read.

Jim read the manuscript and called back within a week. I took the phone call for Matt to say that he was in treatment that afternoon and could not come to the phone. Jim asked me to tell Matt that his poems were good, that he liked them a lot. "Tell him," Jim said, "I think he writes like an Indian." Matt's spirits were lifted for the first time in months.

On one visit, Lois and Jim brought a venison steak for Matt, a gift from Montana he relished. After the first of that year, Jim came to teach a semester at the University of Washington. Out of his warm concern for Matt, Jim came to talk to Matt several times a week. In those last hard months for Matt, Jim talked about the background of the novel he was writing, *Fools Crow*. Jim took Matt far from the hospital works in those hours.

When the treatments were finished without good results, it was time to take Matt home. The morning we were to leave, I was delayed in traffic. I walked into Matt's room to find Jim on his knees, tying Matt's shoelaces for him, smiling and talking as he did.

* * *

My family had had a cabin in the South Fork of the Teton River, west of Choteau, Montana, since 1937. Lois and Jim joined us there for many good times. They came to know the people with whom my brother and I had grown up. These people were the descendants of the Métis—French/Chippewa Cree—who had emigrated from Manitoba to settle in the canyon in the 1870s and 1880s. Lois and Jim very graciously came with us to visit the Bruno family one autumn day. The Métis family felt honored to meet Jim, whom they knew as the author of *Winter in the Blood*. Some years earlier, I had brought Marie Bruno, the big reader in the family, a copy of the novel. After she read the novel, she thanked me eagerly. She said, "This is the first true story."

* * *

One evening in the late eighties, when Jim had published *Fools Crow* and was about to publish *The Indian Lawyer*, we gathered at our house at the round oak table for supper. We were eleven: a teacher I had worked with at the Salish-Kootenai tribal high school and her husband, a young Salish student from British Columbia who was living with us at the time, three young Indian women I had come to know in an Indian Studies class at the university, one with a baby, Lois and Jim, and my daughter and I. All of my guests knew Jim's work, and it meant clean air to them. They wanted to meet him. We had talked and laughed and eaten for a good while when Jim began speaking in a warm, firm voice as an Elder might. They listened and said afterward they would always remember that night with Jim. And I will always remember too because with almost the same gravity in which he had been speaking, he turned to me and said, "You cooked the meat just right."

Missoula Remembers James Welch

DEBRA MAGPIE EARLING
University of Montana

Some people, I thought, will never know how pleasant it is to be distant in a clean rain, the driving rain of a summer storm. It's not like you'd expect, nothing like you'd expect.

James Welch, *Winter in the Blood*

In the first dew days of August, Missoula received the blessing of rain, a coolness that brought a sense of peace. A good day followed the rain, the best the valley had seen in a summer of record-high temperatures. And in the quiet early evening of that clean day of August 4, 2003, James Welch passed away at the age of sixty-two. Barbara Theroux of Fact and Fiction Books in Missoula described the wake of his death as a stillness that holds a rush of memories.

When I was asked to write a tribute to the memory of James Welch, I immediately thought of the Missoula writers' community. I began compiling a long list of contemporary writers in this town, but then I stopped. Missoula is a multifaceted community. And I kept thinking about what one person had said: "We are all trying to process what the passing of Jim Welch means to us as individuals, to our community, and to the world. We're trying to comprehend all that we have lost."

I have been sitting with that idea over this long week. How do we comprehend our loss? How does one community pay tribute to a man the world will long remember? Years earlier Richard Hugo, Welch's teacher and friend, predicted the lasting influence of James Welch.

Hugo's poem titled "Letter to Welch from Browning" carries the haunting message "I'll never see you quite the same. Your words will ring like always on the page."

Last week the media buzzed with the news of James Welch's death. The world beyond our small place here mourns the death of a man we dearly loved. James Welch was one of our own. He belonged to us. We claimed him and were astonished that this gentle genius claimed us too. "You connected with him, because he connected with you," that same friend explained. We were proud that James Welch was "Jim" to us.

"What people may not know is how generous Jim Welch was," the author's longtime friend Margaret Kingsland wrote to me. A teacher at Hellgate High School, recalls Jim speaking to sophomores in his class. "Jim's quiet authority captured them," he said. Others spoke of Welch's benevolence, how he gave of his time and never asked for payment. Jim taught at Two Eagle River School in Pablo, Montana. Many young Indian writers say James Welch has opened the door for them, and not just because he was a writer that others knew but because he was a man who made them feel that they were known.

I spoke with a waitperson named Bobbi who remembered Jim and his wife, Lois. "Together, they glowed," she told me. "I knew his work, but I did not know him personally. Still, the beauty of his insides shone on his face," Bobbi said, then looked away, visibly moved by the memory James Welch had inspired. "I've been trying to think just what he had. . . . He was so kind, so lovely to interact with. I wish I would have told him so."

KPAX's Ian Marquand expressed his heartfelt desire to hear Jim reading a chapter from a new book. "I want to hear that voice . . . see that smile . . . hear that laugh one more time." Strangers touched my arm, leaned closer to tell me their remembrance of James Welch. He was humble, gracious, kind, brilliant, funny. His writing defined "high lonesome." Daniel Kemmis, director of the Center for the Rocky Mountain West, wrote, "Montana and the world are poorer for no longer having the benefit of Jim Welch's remarkable way of speaking the truth but richer for having read his words, for having known the simple goodness of his heart."

I believe stories have the power to heal individuals and communities, so I searched for the story I hoped would help a community say goodbye to James Welch. But this time, that story would not be spoken to me; I told myself.

Then Margaret Kingsland shared a story of Jim that had returned to her again and again. It is the story I longed for: During the celebration of the Centennial of Fort Belknap, James Welch was honored by his tribe. "I can see him and Lois as they lead the dance processional," she said quietly. "I can see the line of people growing behind him, his friends and relatives stepping in to join him. I can hear the voices of the drummers listing. I can see the whole tribe as they fill the room. And he leads that procession onward." Jim describes his meaningful relationship with that place when he writes of the Little Bighorn battlefield:

> The Little Bighorn Valley reminds me a lot of . . . the Fort Belknap Reservation, where my family had our ranch. And we considered that valley a beautiful place to raise families, to run cattle, to grow alfalfa and bluejoint . . . Imagine . . . an immense campground filled with eight thousand people . . . relatives . . . then imagine old ones, the keepers of the stories, as they visit with one another, recounting war honors or joking or teasing a young one who is too full of himself.[1]

"The man who wrote so often about returning home had returned home," Margaret finished.

In my imagination, I am standing to honor the processional James Welch inspired. I stand out of respect. I stand to let a great man pass.

NOTES

This article first appeared in the *Missoula Independent*, September 14, 2003.

1. James Welch, with Paul Stekler, *Killing Custer* (New York: W. W. Norton, 1994).

Backed into the Wind, Clean-Limbed and Patient

DEIRDRE McNAMER
University of Montana

When *Winter in the Blood* was published in 1974, James Welch was a thirty-four year old who had written some wonderful poems that not enough people knew much at all about. A few blinks later, he was more or less famous. *Winter in the Blood* was a "nearly flawless" novel, a "brilliant" work of art, said the big-guns in the review business. And they were right. It is a novel that was, and remains, gorgeous, heart-breaking and finally, seriously, very funny.

In 1974 a lot of us were in our twenties and still feeling our way toward the shape and pattern of our adult lives. Some of us thought we might, perhaps, become writers, that it was, perhaps, a possibility for us. Others of us—I was one—did not have much of an idea about where we were in any grand or ungrand sense, and we would not, for many more years, have a hundred pages of fiction that we could call our own. But some of us had grown up on Montana's northern plains, as Jim did, and now lived in Missoula, where he did, and were lucky enough to know him as a friend.

When you knew Jim apart from his work, you saw that he functioned—in his person, in his being—as living proof that brilliance has virtually nothing to do with talking about it, that success has virtually nothing to do with talking about it.

Aspiring writers who do not have a Jim Welch in their lives can easily get the message that reputations are made and preserved by jostling loudly for advantage: putting yourself out there, flattering the potentially helpful, dissing the no-counts or the competition, saying things you do not mean, affecting an arrogance you do not feel, creating a persona that charms or intimidates and tends to get quoted.

I had the sense that all of that to Jim was just . . . sort of funny. It was like his big dog Ned charging around a gathering to say hi and wag his long tail and steal the cheese if he could. You laugh, you grab your drink, but you certainly do not take Ned's behavior as any sort of lesson in how anyone but a literal big dog ought to operate.

There is a word you do not hear much any more. Modesty. To be modest is to be free from ostentation, says the fourth, best definition in my dictionary. *Free* from it.

It means also, I think, free to savor, without explanation or apology, what might be called the day's ordinary pleasures. Ordinary pleasures in a familiar, well-loved place. As Jim savored them. Though of course pleasures are never ordinary when you come to them knowing in your bones what their utter absence can feel like.

Jim liked to have Lois, his wife, at one end of the table and himself at the other and a bunch of talky, smart-alecky story addicts connecting the two ends. He liked the amplitude and grace of their house, and their yard, and he liked to walk with Lois back to that house at night, behind the footpads of one big dog or another over the years.

Walk back. And then—at one o'clock in the morning or thereabouts, *in the dead vast and middle of the night*—go to work. Until five, or thereabouts. That time on the far, far side of the waking, ordinary, detailed day. That time of the deepest quiet.

I think of him then, and I see a light behind a window, and I see also a horse in a cold wind on the night prairie, the way it stands there, backed into the wind, clean-limbed and patient, head dropped a little, seeming almost to listen.

I think there may have been times, maybe many, when Jim in those otherworldly hours just *listened.*

And he heard a fence humming in the sun. And Long Knife's hair bristling against his collar.

He heard Fools Crow chant with his eyes closed, the rhythm like a heartbeat, as he rubbed sweetgrass smoke over the out-of-his-body boy.

"I was as distant from myself as a hawk from the moon." He heard a young man say that.

He heard the squeak of leather and the bark of a dog, then hundreds of seizers on the march, each with a long gun, their horses snorting white smoke in the cold air.

He heard travois poles make a hissing sound in the dirt and then, from the front of the band, some braves begin to sing.

And then a whole valley alive with singing.

He heard a barmaid without a cigarette blow a smoke ring and tell a customer she might be from the West Coast but not Seattle. "I wouldn't be from Seattle," he heard her say, "for all the rice in China."

Missing Jim

NEIL McMAHON

When I was taking fiction writing classes from Bill Kittredge back in the 1970s, he used to talk about the difficulty of "rendering the ineffable." It's relatively easy to describe people, objects, places, actions, and some basic emotions (like the jolt of fear you'd get if you opened your mailbox and realized there was a rattlesnake inside). But putting more subtle thoughts and feelings on the page effectively is one of the greatest challenges a writer faces.

Jim Welch was a master at it, but that's not what I'm trying to get at. Instead, I'm trying to explain how difficult it is for me to write about him. He's the ineffable here.

I've put off this piece again and again, which is very unlike me, looking for a way to do him justice. I haven't succeeded. I'm most honored to be invited to write this, but I hate writing about him in the past tense. I was incredibly lucky to know him and I loved him dearly, as did all his friends. I've never known a more wonderful human being. He was great-hearted, generous, brilliant, humble, and funny as hell. I can hear his laugh in my head clear as day, but I'd give anything to hear it again for real. He had a *presence*, so steady and understated that we all took it for granted—like air—yet so powerful that we depended on it heavily.

But none of that conveys the man himself or the sheer pleasure of being around him. The best I can think of to do is mention a few things, with no particular relationship to one another and in no particular order.

Jim was remarkable for his gentleness, but he was very strong, with a very tough side. For openers, he spent his early childhood on the Blackfeet and Fort Belknap reservations—hard enough in itself. To go from there to the University of Montana took tremendous courage, and it took a lot more to face the rigorous work and risks of learning to write world-class poetry and fiction.

He served for several years on the State of Montana Board of Pardons and Paroles, dealing with dangerous criminals and knowing that they'd be enraged, and might even come seeking revenge, if their appeals were turned down. He was especially effective with Native American inmates, who understood that he was sympathetic to them, but that they couldn't bullshit or intimidate him.

And there's a famous story (I was reluctant to tell it because it's not mine to tell, but Lois wants me to, because maybe it otherwise wouldn't appear here) about a big-time East Coast critic who savaged one of his novels in a review then, after finding out how revered Jim was, sent an emissary to try to make friends.

Jim's answer went, "I wouldn't walk across the street to watch him eaten by wild dogs."

On the sweeter side, Jim and Lois had the mutual good fortune to hook up, and that was what really made it all work—two very smart, complicated, and outwardly different people meshing in a way I've rarely seen. I don't think there's any doubt that without her, he would have been much more prone to the self-destructive side that many writers have. In turn, he introduced her to a world that was foreign and even threatening but where now she's very much at home.

They threw frequent parties (she still does), where you'd hang out in the living room or backyard with your best friends and come away feeling like your inner batteries had been recharged.

Once Lois and Jim met my wife, Kim, and me in Livingston, Montana, and treated us to an exquisite four-star restaurant dinner. But the next morning Jim must have woken up with a boyhood hunger. He led us firmly past the cafes serving brioche and latte on to a railroad diner, where we tore into liver and onions, greasy sausage, and eggs over easy. We (he and I, anyway) walked out chewing toothpicks and belching happily.

There was an afternoon a few years back (although it doesn't seem nearly that long ago) when they invited me to help put together a set of patio furniture (in spite of the fact that I'd almost destroyed their kitchen on a whiskey-fueled night years before that, trying to adjust a cabinet door). It was one of the most pleasant times I've ever spent. The best way I can describe it is that while we bolted the table and chairs together, we were all just who we were—warts, failings, craziness, and love were understood but never conscious.

I'll close by saying that I won't talk about Jim's books as such—that's been done better by others. But if you want to get to know this great man, read the record he left us through untold thousands of hours that he spent searching his own heart and putting it on the page, word by word.

Finding an Indian Poet

SIMON J. ORTIZ
University of Toronto

The following is taken from correspondence between Simon Ortiz and the editor on November 1, 2005.

Kate,

Thank you. For your persistence. Somebody mentioned Jim Welch recently, but I can't remember who. And I thought then, Hmmmmm, oh yeah, Kate Shanley is doing a *SAIL* issue, and maybe I should write something.

Well, so here you are in the next breath . . .

Would an informal-sounding memory piece be alright? I think I could do something like that. It'll be interesting to me anyway. Geesuz, I think it was 1967-68 when I was asking around for Indian poets. Indian poets? You mean poetry written by Indians, right?

I thought I was the only one doing it!

Well, I knew of the young poets at the Institute of American Indian Art (IAIA) beginning to barely surface in the modern world. By the way, I just met James McGrath recently in Santa Fe at the Lannan Readings and Conversations event I did with Joy Harjo and Leslie Marmon Silko. McGrath and his wife, T. D. Allen, were teachers and mentors of the young poets at IAIA in the 1960s when IAIA started. But other than that, there were no poets. Nothing. I mean literally nothing.

Oh, there were poems rendered from musings by non-Indian aficionados of Indian songs and "Indian ways." Usually hokey and corny and hokey and corny. I mean "poetry" was garnered and romanticized and tokenized and Hollywoodized and so forth. Or there was poetry that sounded like Henry Wordsworth Longfellow or James Fennimore Cooper but obviously nothing that sounded genuine and authentic and could be nothing but Indian! Oh, I think there were writings too that came from students at Indian schools, probably beginning in the 1890s, like from Carlisle, Haskell, perhaps Chilocco, written at Indian schools that were usually very sanitized, contrived, and edited so they looked like sweet, sugary, fluffy renderings that no genuine Indian would sincerely claim! Well, I knew there was real poetry out there. I just knew there had to be. And then I heard of James Welch. And then I met Jim. And then I heard and read his poetry. And the world was never the same since.

Will it work?

Simon

Happiness That Sleeps with Sadness

DAVID L. MOORE
University of Montana

More than twenty-five years ago when he did a reading in Sioux City, Iowa, I first met Jim Welch and his wife, Lois, and I have been grateful to get to know them over the decades. Even during that first meal we shared in a café afterward, I felt a rare, confidential mix of challenge and affection from them both. It seemed to be their implicit challenge to meet the highest standards of expression and honesty, while they both gave their quiet approval and affection for whatever efforts I could make in that direction. They seemed perfectly matched to support each other that way, to encourage good writing and honest speaking. I hope we can all help Lois now.

Jim always dodged superlatives, but I can say that he was one of the least sentimental and most sensible people I ever encountered. He was genuinely the least romantic and the most relentlessly realistic person, but at the same time he was so fully engaged and caring. Somehow he managed to be both penetratingly astute and nonjudgmental. His immediate warmth and chipmunk smile were driven by lion eyes that both sparkled and burned. He looked at the world and at suffering with so little self-pity and so much spontaneous feeling.

His words, of course, were thus constantly surprising, concise, piercing. From the first line in his first book, his language shakes with a strength that, for lack of a better phrase, might be called hardheaded tenderness. It gives his lines a constant edge of polar ultimates, of life and death. And he faced even death with a straightforward clarity. A few weeks before he died, my wife, Kate, and I had Jim and Lois over for dinner, and I asked Jim what he was working on these days, whether he was continuing the sequel to *Charging Elk*. He said casually that he was not taking on any big projects, now that he did not have much time.

Lois explained a few days after he died that when Jim was deep in writing a book, especially *Fools Crow*, it was as though he lived in that other world, interacting with everyone else politely but perfunctorily. She thought that in those last few months he did not want to disappear into that writing world and that he chose instead to interact and to stay close to his friends and family.

He embodied that hardheaded tenderness. In his expression, he gave that impossible balance a moving literary form. Toward the end of *Fools Crow*, the narrator describes a way of dealing with the pain of history as "a happiness that sleeps with sadness." That is what we get to live with now: happiness to have heard his voice, sadness that Jim is gone.

A Tribute to James Welch

WILLIAM WETZEL

Growing up on the Blackfeet Indian Reservation, I always knew I wanted to have a creative career. From before I can accurately recall, my sentiments leaned toward becoming a writer, filmmaker, or anything in the arts that would allow me to express myself. My hero was John F. Kennedy. Of course, I wanted to be president of the United States like him, but I was also intrigued that Kennedy was a Pulitzer Prize–winning writer. Now this was a goal! A novelist president! A presidential novelist!

Most of my life, I hoped to leave my home, forget about my past, and write great screenplays, essays, and novels. Being an Indian was more of a hindrance than anything else. I needed life experience. I needed to see the world. New York. Los Angeles. Seattle. Traveling through Europe and everywhere else I could think of. These would be events to write about. Stories to tell. Who wanted to read about Indians anyway? Who would read anything written by some nobody from Cut Bank, Montana? The thought of living in a big city as a famous writer was so compelling to a little Indian farm hick from Montana that I nearly emoted tears at the precious thought.

I spent most of my life writing poems about loves I never had. A broken heart that was not mine. My stories consisted of places I had never been. I wrote about sunrises and sunsets, peoples and cultures I never saw or knew anything about. I never imagined anybody would want to read anything about the Montana Hi-line or Blackfeet Indians.

The first James Welch novel I ever read was *Winter in the Blood*. This was the story of a Blackfeet Indian, lost in life, struggling for an identity and tormented by visions of his past. A novel of extraordinary beauty, tinged with pain, yet wrought with the clarity of contemporary Indian life. Up until this novel, I never identified with most characters in Indian literature. But this was real. I knew people similar to the unnamed narrator; I saw them every day. Maybe I was a little like him myself. This novel changed my life and my art forever.

Wind blowing over my parents' farm. Snow blanketing the landscape. Mountains in the distance overlooking a vast plain. The tinny taste of snowflakes stinging the tip of my tongue. I hear singing. Dancing. Voices calling stories in the night. Here I am, in the waking hours, envisioning at my dining table, but not there—in another world. Images scorched into my eyes from a place far away. Insomnia grips me. Holds me tight. I cannot sleep when language haunts me, when allure seethes inside my bones, when my pen has stories to tell.

When James Welch was attending the University of Montana, his writing professor pulled him aside to his office and questioned his knowledge of poetry. Until then, Welch wrote rhyming poems about "majestic mountains and wheeling gulls." He wrote of an ocean he had never seen. Later in his one work of nonfiction, Welch mentioned how he always wanted to move to New York or someplace in another world far away from an Indian reservation. He wanted to be famous, to achieve literary greatness. Welch did not want to be an Indian writer but a writer who happened to be an Indian. "The mere thought," he said, "was nearly enough to move me to tears." Now his professor, the legendary poet Richard Hugo, challenged him to write about what he knew, about where he came from. When Welch said he was an Indian, Hugo said, "Go ahead, write about the reservation, the landscape, the people." And so this is what he did.[1]

My deep impression of the Blackfeet Reservation is one of bleakness. Hopelessness. I had constantly felt my home was a place where dreams have been left to die, a location in which the populace was rife with alcoholism, drug addiction, and poverty. The winters are harsh and unforgiving, the employment scarce, and the culture roiling in torment. But somewhere in all this is an undeniable charm, an allure that held captive, and still does, a young boy's imagination. James Welch made me understand the connection and dichotomy of this world.

Deep down, writing about the world I was born into was meaningful. Inevitable. The first time I called Welch and asked him for advice on some stories of mine, he was warm and genuine and encouraged me to write about the same things Richard Hugo told him to write about over thirty years ago. And so this is what I have done.

On August 4, 2003, at age sixty-two, James Welch died of a heart attack at his home in Missoula, Montana, after a long battle with lung cancer. Jim was an internationally acclaimed novelist, winner of the Los Angeles Times Book Award for his masterpiece *Fools Crow*, and was knighted by France in 2000 for his contributions to their culture through his work. I know him as a childhood friend of my father and uncles and as a friend who encouraged me to follow the same path that he did. For the last few years, I have carried around in my wallet a newspaper clipping from when he received his honors from the French government. I carry this for luck, inspiration, and to acknowledge that a man who came from humble beginnings can accomplish so much by simply writing about the small world he grew up in. The same world I grew up in as well. For this I am forever indebted to him.

NOTES

1. James Welch, Introduction to Ken Lopez—Bookseller, third Native American literature catalog, http://www.lopezbooks.com/articles/welch.html.

Trickster of Literacy

STEVE HAWLEY
University of Montana

When James Welch died, the matter of his passing was discussed in an inadvertently comic mode in Missoula at the gym where I used to work out in the mornings. A small coffee and juice bar served as an informal gathering spot to glance at the day's headlines. Someone would read a few lines aloud from a front-page story or, more commonly, raise a comment on the dismal turn of events portrayed on CNN, and the rest of the men—this was an exclusively male ritual—would offer an opinion if so moved. These were generally decent, conservative, no-nonsense, middle-aged men who did not waste a lot of time reading books, with one exception.

One-legged Simms, a shrewd businessman with a liberal streak and a tricksterlike penchant for suckering others into his discussions, usually played host, hogging the newspaper, murmuring a few words from the front page, and adding his own editorial comments, often irreverently baiting the clientele at the bar with an acerbic remark about the absurdity of the Iraq war or the hypocrisy of Rush's drug addiction. Though the arguments Simms incited sometimes escalated into shouts in the parking lot, he spoke with impunity, for the simple reason that no one wanted to get into a brawl with a one-legged guy, certainly an unwinnable proposition from any opponent's standpoint.

"Lotta big names in town for the memorial of James Welch," Simms reported nonchalantly that February morning.

"Givin' up protesting the war, huh Simms?" said Todd, a born-again urban cowboy who worked out in a tank top, factory-faded jeans, and horseman's boots.

"Your back hurts again, doesn't it, Todd?" observed Simms. "You want to know why? It's because you're fat. You insist on wearing those fruity boots, then you come in here, work your biceps and your jaws, and then you go home and eat all the fatty food your wife cooks. When are you going to get an *aerobic* workout? If you're not going to use the legs, then at least give me one of them."

"Welch, I think I got his book from someone at church," said Slick, a tight-lipped CPA.

"Welch's?" Simms asked, surprised.

"Yeah, I got that too, called *Inside My Gut* or something like that," chimed in Todd, his face a shade more crimson than usual, pretending to ignore the verbal lashing from Simms.

"Didn't know he died," said the electrician, sipping his coffee.

"Didn't know he's from Montana," someone else said.

"Probably he's not," said the sporting goods store manager. "Every one of these rich CEOs makes a bundle and then buys themselves a spread on the Front or on the Madison. Then they pretend they've lived here their whole lives."

Simms's eyes lit up; he kicked me under the bar with his prosthetic foot. "Says here Tom Brokaw was there."

"No surprise there," said Slick. "GE owns NBC, so he came to pay his respects to the boss."

"Knighted by the French," smiled Simms.

"Figures," said the barista with disdain, rolling his eyes.

"Says here he's Blackfeet Indian too." A few furtive glances came Simms's way, then passed.

"Who woulda guessed," said the electrician, rising as he spoke, glancing at his watch, slugging his coffee, prompting the procession out toward the day.

Of course, former General Electric executive *Jack* Welch has proven to be neither honest (a development that belies the title of his 2001 best seller, *Straight from the Gut*) nor Indian. By contrast, James Welch owns both a full measure of brutal honesty and Blackfeet Indian identity and would not have needed a kick from Simms's fake leg to get a laugh out of the misdirection at the gym that morning.

Bill Kittredge eulogized his friend Jim Welch as a trickster figure. Of course, tricksters come in every shape and size, with a myriad of modus operandi. While Simms's antics always involved an initial deception, baiting a trap laid in a subsistence hunt for nourishment in the cruel banalities of the business world, James Welch sought sustenance in the comic irony that truth really is stranger than fiction, a trickster reversal that will continue breathing laughter into good, true stories at the least likely crossroads.

Remembering James Welch's Poetry

GAIL TREMBLAY
Evergreen State University

I first became aware of James Welch's work when Richard Hugo selected a number of poems by American Indian writers for the *American Review of Poetry*, and then in 1971, when *Riding the Earthboy* 40 was published, I bought the book and read and reread it. It was a book that moved me and made me feel less alone in the world. While I loved Jim's novels and taught them, as a poet, I always wished there had been more books of poetry. I recognize that no one really makes a living as a poet, and for Welch, as one of the great fiction writers in late-twentieth and early-twenty-first-century American letters, it would not have made sense to indulge in producing books of poetry, but he was such a fine and gifted poet that I have always wished that there were more poems by him somewhere in the world.

The thing that I have always loved about poems is the way that they can use a few words to take one on a great journey toward a revelation. This is certainly true of my favorite poems by James Welch. I think of his poem "Getting Things Straight" and the way it starts with a question: "Is the sun that same drab gold?" (49). The poem proceeds to pose nine more questions to make readers reflect on the nature of raptors and their lessons for humans. It opens the reader to possibilities and insists that the answer must always be personal. In the second line and part of the third line, we meet the raptor, "The hawk—is he rising, circling, / falling above the field?" I love the way Welch uses rising and falling and creates the soft whispering by repeating the *f* sounds with "falling above the field." That choice of word "falling" makes the hawk seem somewhat vulnerable in the beginning of the poem and makes the transformation at the end of poem stronger.

Then Welch takes us away from the bird; he asks, "And the rolling day, / it will never stop?" The choice of "rolling" echoes the hawk's "circling" in an interesting way at the same time it sweeps us into a wider space, since day marks time on an earth that is rolling around a sun moving in an ever expanding universe. And this question mark makes us reflect on what could otherwise be read as a dishonest statement, since we know that the motion must go on, so days come and go, and that our sun will someday explode, that both the rolling day and the rolling of days will stop even though we desire a constant and secure world that can never really exist. Then Welch asks his most abstract and existential question: "It means nothing?" Again he is refusing by using a question mark to make this a statement, and so he presents and opens another possibility in three short words. Next, he makes reference to the past and place, and asks us,

> Will it end the way history ended when
> the last giant climbed Heart Butte, had a vision
> came back to town and drank himself
> sick?

I believe that what Welch is asking here is whether it is possible to have visions in this modern age and not come back and drink. Is the old context in which visions were normal parts of existence in culture gone forever? Can Indigenous people bear to have visions in a colonial world that defines Indigenous as "primitive" and visions as superstitions? Do even the last visionary giants need to medicate themselves with drink, and where does that leave the rest of us? Welch then returns us to the raptor. He makes in two declarative sentences the following observations:

> The hawk sees a mouse.
> Wheeling, falling, stumbling to a stop,
> he watches a snake ribbon quickly
> under a rock?

Then he asks the reader, "What does it mean?" He then observes, "He flashes his wings to the sun, bobs / twice and lifts, screaming / off the ground." This language telescopes the description of the hawk diving for the kill, failing to make a kill, and flying away hungry. Welch then asks about how the hawk makes meaning of his act, "Does it mean this to him, / the mouse, a snake, the dozen angry days / still rolling since his last good feed?" Then Welch asks us, "Who offers him a friendly meal? / Am I strangling in his grip? / Is he my vision?" In nineteen short lines he moves us to reflect on our relation to a bird and the possibility that the bird might, if we observe it carefully, become the vehicle to understanding something about the nature of the world—a vision. He opens us to question what it is possible to know and understand.

Because I find such journeys rich in possibility, even after all these years of reading, I come back to Welch's poems and savor carefully chosen words that lead me down roads I find familiar. When Welch asks, "Am I strangling in his grip?" he is letting us know that if this is a vision, it preys on us in complex ways, and however he or we answer that final question the author opens for himself, neither nature nor its lessons are simple.

After all these years, I still wish that there were more poems lurking in some space amid James Welch's things, and I am sorry he is gone from us and will not be writing more. His slim volume of verse moves me, and I thank him for bringing these poems into the world, so I can travel in them.

WORKS CITED

Welch, James. *Riding the Earthboy* 40. 1971. Reprint, New York: Penguin, 2004.

Keening Woman and Today

James Welch's Early Unpublished Novel

Thomas Orton

It was most likely in the spring of 1966 that the late American Indian novelist James Welch wrote his first novel, predating his first published fiction by eight years. The titleless, hand-corrected typescript, stored in his Missoula home for many years, is 114 pages long and unfinished. The book is playful and experimental the way warm-ups sometimes are. It is filled with lively images and humorous dialogue. Its young author's mind is alive with metaphor, his eye and ear demonstrably sharp. This is a truly formative work with touches of early brilliance that are traceable in the mature novels and poetry.

The book shares with Welch's first published novel, *Winter in the Blood*, the Montana setting and the first-person narration. In most of the book, the Indian subject matter is absent. The book contains neither the crystalline emotional energy of Welch's poems nor the gritty starkness of his early published fiction. Also missing, at least from the first part of the manuscript, is a strong physical sense of place, descriptions of landscape, and the awareness of the natural world so much a part of Welch's later work.

In light of Welch's published work, the tone and the diction at the beginning of this book are completely unexpected. The hero, Jimmie Jarrell, is a white San Franciscan who, having just finished college in Missoula, is planning to have an adventure. While in Welch's later fiction the writing is pared down and bracing, this book opens with the breezy tone of a Dawn Powell novel—smart, frothy, full of educated urbanity and snappy dialogue. One of Jimmie Jarrell's best friends is named Archie Carrew. Jimmie's girlfriend, Jana, a New Englander, is not beautiful but is witty and quick. They all call one another "darling" and "my dears." They look down on the "starry-eyed farm boys and girls at the University." Their concerns are mostly sex and having a good time. Westernisms like "powwow," "many moons," and "I'll be a ring-tail polecat" casually punctuate their fad-conscious language. Jimmie is writing a book himself; his novel is "stagnant," which makes him fashionably blocked. The first half of Welch's novel is filled with literary references. The characters talk about the works of Shakespeare, Emerson, and Dostoyevsky, the "Pleasure Dome," Mallarme and the "Symbolistes," and "Shaw's creative evolution."

In expatriot Jimmie, Welch is trying on a different persona, an altogether healthy, helpful, and necessary exercise for a writer and one that develops empathy. He is attempting to discover what it would be like not to be an Indian. It is likely that Welch intended this book as a satire, though it is difficult to be sure since the tone changes dramatically later on and the original conceit is never fully fleshed out. Whether or not he meant to poke fun at supposedly urbane outsiders condescending to live in "provincial" Montana, the author may well have been exploring his ambivalence about his own place in the West.

Jimmie Jarrell has just received two thousand dollars, "a gift from my mother who is very wealthy and very tight. The filthy lucre of a speculating mind is mine for the asking now." His mother wants him "to have the advantages in life which only money can give." Welch is drawn to Jarrell as the sort of lucky American male who blends into the culture at large, who is a member of the club, who does not stand apart from American life as Indians do.

The first sign that Jimmie has more depth than first appears is his intense interest in the horses that he watches running outside the window of his home. They ran for "no REASON," Jimmie insists, and later he hears "their crashing hoofs echo through my psyche for hours on end."

Jimmie decides to begin his postcollege adventure with a drive north to Havre to visit his friend Vinnie and Vinnie's voluptuous girlfriend, Cherry, whom Jimmie dislikes. On this drive, the natural world begins to find its way into the narrative. "Somewhere out in a hayfield, a pheasant garbles a message of love or hunger or a challenge, ignored by the sinister magpies, western Poe ravens, dozing on rotten fence posts." The tone turns somewhat more reverential in these descriptions, which seem to seize Jimmie in the same mysterious way that the running horses did. "There is a hollow sadness," Jimmie tells us, "as the shadows merge with dusk." One morning he wakes up hearing "a meadowlark singing loops of notes against the high basement window."

The writing grows more lyrical, lilting, and freewheeling, unconcerned with syntax. "It's a farmer's morning and the fields are filled with popping wheat, green grow the lilacs of town[,] and God sent this morning to scorn my lethargy." Welch shows an ear for dialogue here as well. Jimmie's friend Vinnie tells another man, "I envy you, Herb. Really do. Beautiful wife, fine mind, decent; you know what I mean? I mean decent like you're such a simple soul that all the crap you put up with is meaningless."

Humor plays a role here, as it often does in Welch's later novels. Vinnie proudly shows Jimmie three trout he caught, which he tells us, "would have turned up missing in a fish bowl." Jimmie and his brilliant friend Vinnie figure that "if you took actual paperback pages and laid them side by side, [Vinnie] would have read around the world two and a half times while I would have read to Peabody, Massachusetts." Another of Vinnie and Jimmie's friends, Fat Mike, "was the fattest baby in a small town in eastern Montana. He writes home occasionally to see if his record still stands (which it does)." Jimmie goes to the library and reads Emerson. To keep from getting "boggled down," he goes "over to Cherry's side of the library where I find a book on 5 mistakes to avoid in lovemaking (one of which is to leave the phone on the hook)."

In Havre Jimmie shaves off his intellectual's beard and outfits himself in western style, buying a cowboy hat and boots. Arguably, American culture considers the cowboy one of the most truly American males, whereas Indians are relegated to the opposite end of the spectrum. Again, while burlesquing the western man, Welch also seems fascinated by a concept of freedom that might not be available to Indians.

In Havre the narration sheds more of its bantering tone, becomes more serious and poetic. "Hordes of bad dreams settle here," Jimmie tells the reader, "and people choose the worst." A woman has "eyes the color of burnt magpie wings." At the beginning of the novel, Montana as a setting is just a word, but now a sense of the physical surroundings begins to emerge. With Vinnie, Jimmie crosses the Milk River, which is

> dirty and lazy beneath the narrow bridge; as we enter a neighborhood of corner stores and scab barbers, kids in striped, holey t-shirts ride patched together bikes in the hot damp evening. Vinnie turns the gaudy Chrysler off the main street down a gravel chuckhole road lined with shacks, dead car bodies[,] barking dogs and last year's leaves piled against weathered fences. He pulls over into an alley behind a warehouse and stops before a prefab duplex which squats in abeyance at the foot of a bluff, runneled and eroded by forgotten floods.

At this point in the book, Vinnie and Cherry introduce Jimmie to Monica, who is a former nun, which at first appears to fit the satire theme. But Jimmie's first meeting with Monica triggers an avalanche of deeply felt images:

> shards of a whisper draining my sleep can't produce the purple light and the tigers who walk the beach turn to butter in polar light but [t]his is her hand proffered by Divine Manifestation, even the knuckles are wax, even blood is flowing uphill to her heart, even my veins.
>
> "You must be Jimmie[.]"

These images are excited, inscrutable, and feverish. The sentences lose structure, but the emotional impact is clear.

Jimmie falls tenderly in love with Monica, and the scenes with her are the best of the book. Love transforms ordinary moments that might have bored the old breezy, ironic Jimmie. Monica asks,

> "Would you like some cinnamon toast. It's my specialty?"
>
> "Well, yes," I say and follow her so I can watch her move, so divinely simple in the the [*sic*] small slant-roof kitchen made for rainy loneliness.

Together they watch a storm,

> One by one, the florescent jags march to the east followed by

> the wind and rain and we are left finally with the oppressive stillness of our own tongues. A haze across the bridge suggests downtown lights and now the little boys comb the nightly lawns for nightcrawlers, naked and obscene. Vinnie stands and stretches and tells us of a star far to the west. Monica stirs and laughs . . . the relief is sudden and we receive life in our damp bones.

In the midst of these scenes of early love with Monica, a remarkable passage occurs. Monica comes down with pneumonia, and Jimmie, who has stayed on in Havre to write, begins nursing her. His narration in this section dips into stream of consciousness. In one of these passages, Jimmie recalls portaging a canoe in Minnesota on a Fourth of July, then paddling to an island. "I was not surprised that the closer I got to the island, the more unusual would become the rhythm and the color of the water, which became boiling blood." He is

> listening for something I would recognize although I had heard it only once before and that a long long time ago. I pulled the canoe up on the bank and ran my fingers along the bottom of the red-stained hull and tasted, not blood but tears, salty and sad. It was then I discovered that the tears were indelible, left not a trace on my handkerchief, seeped into my skin a sorrow intense and vibrated in my tuning fork ear the high falsetto keening of the ancient Indian woman.

The pages at this point in the typescript are no longer numbered, and the text is not broken into paragraphs. In doing away with these road signs, Welch is willing himself to become lost. The whole unfolding scene might be a dream, in light of which it is not difficult to see those bloodlike tears as an image of the recent history of American Indians. Keening Woman enters into a dialogue with a male character, her lover, who is called Today. Jimmie understands himself to be the son of these two. The dialogue, set up on the page like a play script, is contemporary and casual, which does not disguise the fact that this is a joining of past and present.

In the Keening Woman section, Welch embraces himself, his heritage, and his future subject matter. For as much as he may have wanted to distance himself from his own past and future, he knew that it was his and that there would be no running from it. Not many live with that kind of honesty.

Clearly, James Welch learned an enormous amount from writing this book. He never again used words like "antistrophe" or phrases like "loath to admit" and "distaff life" and "the fixative of our mutual respect." He did, however, write many more sentences like "It isn't what someone said but did that drove the thunder back into the mountains."

The book clarified his calling. His true and lasting voice emerged in a hurry. The same spring he wrote this first novel, or possibly the following autumn, he started producing poems at a prodigious rate for Richard Hugo's graduate poetry workshop at the University of Montana. Shortly afterward, he began publishing. He needed very little practice before settling in to write seriously brilliant and original literature.

The differences in maturity, control, and restraint between this first effort and his later work is astounding, but it is not merely a matter of practice. This early book is James Welch's declaration: I am a writer, and I am an Indian. He is putting everyone on notice, including himself. This book is the icon of his decision.

The Strength of Native Women in James Welch's *Winter in the Blood*

PATRICE HOLLRAH
University of Nevada, Las Vegas

Female characters in the literature of James Welch (Blackfeet/Gros Ventre) sometimes seem overshadowed by the principal male characters, and often the titles of the novels are about the male protagonists: the nameless protagonist in *Winter in the Blood* (1976), *The Death of Jim Loney* (1979), White Man's Dog in *Fools Crow* (1986), Sylvester Yellow Calf in *The Indian Lawyer* (1990), and Charging Elk in *The Heartsong of Charging Elk* (2000). However, in Welch's novels the women hold important places and are necessary for the narratives. This essay looks at how the strength of the Native women are an integral part of the tribal context in which, to borrow Stephen Tatum's phrase, Welch's "I" exists (74).

For example, in *The Heartsong of Charging Elk*, the opening and conclusion frame the novel with female emotions. The first sentence speaks to the changes taking place in 1877 for the Lakotas and of the women's feelings, which set the tone: "It was early in the Moon of the Shedding Ponies, less than a year after the fight with the longknives on the Greasy Grass, and the people looked down in the valley and they saw the white man's fort and several of the women wept" (1; italics in the original). In describing the setting, Welch uses the historical aftermath of the death of Gen. George Armstrong Custer at the Battle of the Little Bighorn, also known as the Battle of Greasy Grass Creek, the ensuing surrender of the Lakotas, and the women's feelings about the surrender to convey the sentiment of the people. The women's tears represent the sadness at being forced to obey the white men: "[Charging Elk] understood that his father and the other men would not fight anymore. He understood that his people would not be allowed to go back to the buffalo ranges. They were prisoners" (3). Although the focus might appear to be on the male warriors and the loss of their hunting and way of life, the women's emotions are needed to comment on what happens to the Natives. The novel follows the life of Charging Elk as he travels to France with Buffalo Bill's Wild West show, but the conclusion of the novel returns to thoughts of his mother, thinking of her as she was singing at the opening of the novel:

> He saw his mother in the kitchen, cooking meat for him and Strikes Plenty. He saw her on the travois horse, the tears, as they waited to descend into the valley of Fort Robinson. Then he heard her singing, all of the people singing. "She will be all right," he said. "She will be better off without me. By now, she thinks I am dead for sixteen years. Let her remember me with a loving heart." (437)

Despite a narrative that follows the challenges Charging Elk faces in a foreign country, where he at first does not know the language, he still cares what his mother is feeling and thinking. The woman's emotions are acknowledged as important in his life.

In the same way that the women are necessary in *The Heartsong of Charging Elk*, they are also crucial in *Fools Crow*. P. Jane Hafen (Taos Pueblo), in her essay "Constructing the Center of *Fools Crow*," writes about the complementary function of the female characters:

> *Fools Crow* could be read as the coming of age for the main male character who symbolically represents the historical changes among the Blackfeet peoples. Detailed descriptions of domestic duties and relationships frankly document the difficult lives of Blackfeet women of the 1860s. Careful reading, however, reveals that White Man's Dog can transform only with the complementarity of female characters. The characters reveal the complexity of the human experience: Heavy Shield Woman shows sorrow and purity; Red Paint shows youth, wholeness, and joy; Kills-close-to-the-lake shows temptation, repentance, and change required for survival; Feather woman shows the sacred and mythic power of hope and vision. Language imagery notes the

> unity of the male and female, with the female at the center of this novel. (10)[1]

Hafen illustrates how the female characters are relevant to the journey of masculine transformation for the main character.

A similar transformation takes place in *Winter in the Blood*, the contemporary version of *Fools Crow*. Literary criticisms of *Winter in the Blood* usually focus on the nameless male protagonist, his alienation and reconnection with his Blackfeet heritage. In discussing the narrator's return home to the reservation and eventual discovery of the identity of his Blackfeet grandfather, Yellow Calf, critics also have looked at the role that the female characters play in supporting his journey. Often critics treat the Native women as secondary characters, merely as backdrop against which the main character plays out his coming-of-age role, or perhaps coming-to-terms-with-his-past role would be a better descriptor. His own self-described state of distance acknowledges his lack of connection to his female relatives: "But the distance I felt came not from country or people; it came from within me. I was as distant from myself as the hawk from the moon. And that was why I had no particular feelings toward my mother and grandmother. Or the girl who had come to live with me" (2). A. LaVonne Ruoff writes about the protagonist as a person who feels closer to his deceased father and brother, John First Raise and Mose, respectively, than he does to his living female family members, and she argues that he needs to reconnect with the female principle in order to exorcise the alienation from which he suffers (59). In a tribal structure of gender complementarity, he would need to realize that the women complement him, that their roles are necessary for his health as an individual and as a member of his family and tribe.

A tribal structure of gender complementarity explains, in part, how the Native women are able to hold some of the strong roles in the novel. Consequently, the Native women represent more than what critic Ronald McFarland refers to as "the most frequently recurring 'type' of female character in contemporary Native American writing . . . the 'bar woman'" (148). Often-overlooked female characters in the novel suggest a much broader spectrum of Native women than the most regularly discussed women, the ones whom the unnamed narrator meets in bars and with whom he has one-night stands or short-term sexual relationships: the Cree girl Agnes, "who was thought to be [his] wife" (2), the bar maid in Malta (47), the single mother Malvina (76), and the nursemaid Marlene (116). Additionally, the three women for whom the "I" claims he has no particular feelings—the grandmother, mother, and Agnes—have more power than simply their kinship or romantic relationship to him.

In Barbara Cook's essay on Welch's historical novel *Fools Crow*, she focuses on the economic role that women play and argues that there is "a bilateral position of power between men and women" (449). She states, "Indeed, women are central to the survival of the Blackfeet tribal community that Welch creates and in many ways this strength and centrality provide background for the strength of the women depicted in his more contemporary novels" (441). Cook concludes, "Reflecting on the roles of women fulfilled in the past and their relative position of balance in contemporary Blackfeet society leads to the conclusion that it is the day-to-day functions they performed that enabled cultural survival" (450-51). While Cook notes the "balance needed for survival" (451), she never fully explains the concept of gender complementarity as the underlying basis for the structure of gender relations that allows that "balance" to exist. However, she rightly notes that the strength of women provides the foundation for the roles of women in Welch's contemporary novels.

The strength of women partially originates in a tribal context of gender complementarity, a concept that allows for many variations, as gender roles are social constructs or, more importantly, tribal constructs. In a relatively traditional or historical context, women can perform tasks that normally would be considered men's behaviors within the tribe, and because of special circumstances, such as widowhood or merely living as a single person, they do not seem unusual. Additionally, because people can act with autonomy, making decisions about their own conduct, women can choose to engage in male-gendered behaviors—for example, warrior women—and not seem atypical. While contemporary Native women have survived colonization and the changes it has brought, gender compelmentarity continues to the present day and examples can be found in the construction of literary female characters.

In discussing the traditional female role alternatives of the Piegans of Alberta and Montana, Lakota anthropologist Bea Medicine points out one option that allowed women great latitude in male-gendered behaviors:

> Among the Piegan, there was a small group of women, called "manly-hearted women," whose ambition, boldness, and eroticism contrasted with the prevailing ideal of female submission and reserve. . . . They accorded these women exceptional privileges and prestige in areas typically associated with men. Manly-hearted women excelled in every important aspect of tribal life: property ownership, ceremonialism, and domestic affairs. . . . These women attained wealth by taking on the economic roles typically played by men, and as a consequence they attained a level of self-sufficiency that permitted them independence in other realms as well. (130-31)

The representation of a manly-hearted woman aptly describes Belva Long Knife, the mother of cowboy Raymond Long Knife. Her physical cowboy work challenges any rigid notions of gendered behaviors or occupations:

> Long Knife came from a long line of cowboys. Even his mother, perhaps the best of them all, rode all day, every day, when it came time to round up the cattle for branding. In the makeshift pen, she wrestled calves, castrated them, then threw the balls into the ashes of the branding fire. She made a point of eating the roasted balls while glaring at one man, then another—even her sons, who, like the rest of us, stared at the brown hills until she was done.
>
> Perhaps it was because of this fierce mother that Long Knife had become shrewd in the way dumb men are shrewd. He had learned to give the illusion of work, even to the point of sweating as soon as he put his gloves on, while doing very little. But because he was Belva Long Knife's son and because he always seemed to be hanging around the bar in Dodson, he was in constant demand. (Welch, *Winter* 24)

Belva Long Knife certainly gives the impression of a bold woman who can hold her own with the men through both respect and intimidation. She rides all day, rounds up the cattle for branding, wrestles them to the ground, and castrates them as well as, if not better than, any of the men, and she has no qualms about roasting and eating the testicles. Ruoff sees these acts as an illustration of the female as castrator, and "the economic power of women over men . . . as a less dramatic form of castration" (70). This reading of Belva Long Knife, however, does not allow for any sense of gender complementarity or optional social position, allowing the woman's role and work a valid space within the community. Further, the passage does not read as if the men do not credit her abilities, and, in fact, their respect for her as a "fierce woman" extends to Raymond, whom people willingly hire simply because he is her son. Finally, the narrator speculates that Raymond has learned shrewdness from having such a mother as Belva, which indicates that she has also fulfilled the role of mother in a positive way. Although there is no specific mention of an absent husband, whether due to death, divorce, or desertion, the reader can assume that Belva Long Knife lives as a single parent and as such has made the necessary adaptations to survive economically. In the process, Belva Long Knife has politically empowered herself within the tribe in terms of the influence she has on the community.

Medicine goes on to compare the manly-hearted woman to other "socially sanctioned status positions for women" to illustrate that she is not a "'deviation' but one of several alternative female roles: (1) *ninawaki* (manly woman); (2) *matsaps* (crazy woman); (3) Sun Dance woman; and (4) *ninaki* (chief woman or favorite wife)" (131). The grandmother relates stories from her early life to her grandson and explains how she was the third wife, not the favorite wife, of Standing Bear, a Blackfeet chief (Welch, *Winter* 34). While the grandmother does not state that the chief had a favorite wife, she does note that as the third wife she "sat between his older wives and his daughters," suggesting her place in the order of the family. One can infer that the first wife holds the position of favorite wife, or the "sits-beside-me-wife," and would have special status, duties, and privileges (Medicine 131).

Welch deals with the role of the Sun Dance woman in *Fools Crow*, a woman who in Piegan society represented "the extreme of womanly virtue. Before marriage she was a virgin. She was never unfaithful to her husband, nor did she remarry after his death" (Medicine 132). Although the grandmother in *Winter in the Blood* never has the opportunity to be the Sun Dance woman, certain aspects of her life speak to the role. She never had sexual relations with Standing Bear according to the narrator: "Sometimes she slept with him, though he was almost thirty years older than she was. On those nights, beneath the wooly robes, she snuggled against his large body and sang softly in his ear" (35). She was not yet twenty when she became a widow, and "she had produced no children, had slept with Standing Bear only to whisper her songs" (37). The narrator goes on to say that "she remained a widow for twenty-five years before she met a half-white drifter named Doagie," with whom she lived, though they never married. "Teresa was their only offspring. And it was questioned whether Doagie was her real father or not" (37–38). While the grandmother does not remain a virgin, she was never unfaithful to her husband while he was alive, does not disrespect his memory by remarrying, and never reveals the true father of her daughter, Teresa. Her affair with Yellow Calf was "so solemn and secretive it had not even been rumored" (161). Had Standing Bear lived, there is a good indication that she might have remained a virtuous woman, considered for the Sun Dance woman.

The last of the four socially sanctioned status positions is crazy woman, which Medicine claims carries "special references to sexual promiscuity" (131). Medicine does not explicate this position in terms of Piegan culture but of a Lakota correlate female figure, *witkowin*. She details how "sexual promiscuity . . . was sanctioned through certain types of dreams" (131). If a Lakota woman dreamed of the *Wakinya* (Thunder Beings), she was released "from her commitments to the cultural ideals of virginity or marital fidelity" (131). While there is no one female character in *Winter in the Blood* who dreams of Thunder Beings, there is a proliferation of sexual promiscuity. Also, there is an interesting association with Welch's use of the sound of thunder, "a low rumble," and the "thunderheads" in anticipation of the rain (*Winter* 38). Despite a place for sexually active Blackfeet women in the role of crazy woman, the "virtuous" grandmother hates Agnes because she is Cree, a traditional enemy of the Blackfeet, someone whom she believes drinks too much and is sexually promiscuous (33): the grandmother "plotted ways to slit her throat" (5).

The grandmother's behaviors are consistent with the warrior women. Medicine offers several examples of when women might participate in warrior activities:

> Among the Blackfeet, there appear to have been women who pursued warfare as an extension of their manly inclinations. . . . There were also women, usually childless, who accompanied their spouses on raiding expeditions and who may (or may not) have been actively involved in fighting. . . . And finally, there were women who took on the role of warrior only for a short time and for a specific reason (e.g., to avenge the death of a relative). (133)

The grandmother fits the last description, a woman who wants to take on the role of warrior for the specific purpose of killing Agnes, a Cree enemy: "Though almost a century old, almost blind and certainly toothless, she wanted to murder the girl, to avenge those many sins committed by generations of Crees" (Welch, *Winter* 34).

The grandmother is a strong woman who survived the 1883–84 Starvation Winter and lives to be almost a hundred years old. She finds a way to provide a stepfather, Doagie, for her daughter and to protect her reputation. There is at least one woman, however, who knows that Doagie is not the father of Teresa and communicates this information to the grandson: "The woman who had informed me made signs that he wasn't" (38). This unnamed woman transmits genealogical information that the grandson needs to know to connect to his Blackfeet heritage, echoing other literary females who have communicated this same kind of information to young Native men. For example, Lulu in Louise Erdrich's *Bingo Palace* tells Lipsha that his father is her son, Gerry Nanapush. In this way, strong Native women continue to be the transmitters of tribal cultural information to future generations.

Teresa continues the tradition of strong Blackfeet women. She is economically independent, owning her 360 acres, slaughters animals for food without remorse—like Amos, the pet duck, for Christmas dinner

(18)—and manages the family after the deaths of her son, Mose, her husband, John First Raise, and her mother. Teresa, like her mother, is a survivor. These women fill whatever roles their lives require of them in order to continue. Gender complementarity allows these women to complement their male counterparts in their culture. In connecting with his Blackfeet heritage, in closing the "distance," the son also connects more consciously with that part of his culture that includes the role women play. When Mrs. Ferdinand Horn asks him whether he has brought Agnes back, the narrator lies, "Yes, . . . She's in at the house now. Do you want to see her?" (165). Not only does he want Agnes, but he also knows that he needs her in order to be balanced, to complement him.

NOTES

1. I want to thank P. Jane Hafen for graciously giving me permission to quote from her conference paper.

WORKS CITED

Cook, Barbara. "A Tapestry of History and Reimagination: Women's Place in James Welch's *Fools Crow*." *American Indian Quarterly* 24.3 (Summer 2000): 441–53.

Hafen, P. Jane. (Taos Pueblo). "Constructing the Female Center of *Fools Crow*." Paper presented at the Native American Literature Symposium. Mystic Lake Casino-Hotel, Prior Lake, Minnesota. April 10–13, 2002.

McFarland, Ronald, ed. *James Welch*. Lewiston: Confluence, 1986.

McFarland, Ronald. "Women's Roles in Contemporary Native American Writing and in Welch's *The Death of Jim Loney*." McFarland 147–57.

Medicine, Beatrice. (Lakota). *Learning to Be an Anthropologist and Remaining "Native": Selected Writings*. Urbana: U of Illinois P, 2001.

Ruoff, A. LaVonne. "Alienation and the Female Principle in *Winter in the Blood*." McFarland 59–82.

Tatum, Stephen. "'Distance,' Desire, and the Ideological Matrix of *Winter in the Blood*." *Arizona Quarterly* 46.2 (Summer 1990): 73–100.

Welch, James. (Blackfeet/Gros Ventre). *Fools Crow*. New York: Penguin, 1986.

———. *The Heartsong of Charging Elk*. New York: Doubleday, 2000.

———. *The Indian Lawyer*. New York: W. W. Norton, 1990.

———. *Winter in the Blood*. New York: Penguin, 1974.

Transmitted Trauma and "Absent Memory" in James Welch's *The Death of Jim Loney*

JENNIFER LEMBERG
New York University

There are multiple reasons why the interdisciplinary fields of Holocaust studies and American Indian literary studies have maintained a cautious distance from each other. Wary of critical paradigms that might further "racialist tropes of vanishment," scholars of American Indian literature have hesitated to embrace a discourse of trauma based in Western theoretical models, while Holocaust studies has only recently opened up to broader explorations of the meanings of the event in relationship to other genocides (Vizenor 96; Rothberg 1240). Yet the fields share a central concern with the effort to understand how genocide is understood and represented as "a catastrophic originary event and a recurrent *condition*" (Sanyal 3).[1] In this essay, I argue for their potential to be mutually illuminating through a reading of James Welch's 1979 novel, *The Death of Jim Loney.*

The Death of Jim Loney chronicles the life and death of Loney, the son of a Gros Ventre woman and a white man, who becomes overwhelmed by the need to remember his past in the weeks leading up to Thanksgiving and Christmas. Living in Harlem, Montana, abandoned by his parents, and lacking ties to the Gros Ventres, Loney feels "like an amnesiac searching for the one event, the one person or moment, that would bring everything back" so that he can "see the order in his life" (20). On a quest for memory he will not find, he spends night after night attempting to "think of all the little things that added up to a man sitting at a table drinking wine" (20). With no community to help him in his task and his few remaining family members meeting his efforts with silence or denials, Loney's memory is continuously deferred. He remains burdened by its traces, the continual presence of an absence, like the vision of the dark bird he sees when he is drunk or tired, the meaning of which he cannot discover. The book ends as Loney dies on the Fort Belknap Reservation in what is essentially a suicide: worn down by the larger as well as the quotidian losses he suffers, he is shot by Quinton Doore, a schoolmate of Loney's now distinguished by "a kind of cruelty" and employed by the reservation police (161).

Discussions of *Jim Loney* trace some of the boundaries of American Indian criticism, where American Indian literature is often evaluated according to whether it offers what Gerald Vizenor calls narratives of "survivance" (15), or intellectual and emotional sustenance, and where depictions of the recovery of cultural memory, rather than its depletion, are praised for furthering the project of American Indian cultural renewal. Paul Eisenstein writes that the "omitted history" of Welch's 1974 *Winter in the Blood* creates a "void" in the narrator's "historical consciousness" that functions by "setting the stage for recovery and . . . becoming," but it is uncertain whether Loney's amnesia can be said to work in a similar fashion (12, 6). Comparing *Jim Loney* to other American Indian novels published at the time, such as N. Scott Momaday's *House Made of Dawn* (1968) and Leslie Marmon Silko's *Ceremony* (1977), critics have argued either that, like the protagonists of those works, Loney participates in a ritual that restores him to his tribe (albeit through his death) or that in denying Loney the memory he seeks Welch challenges generic conventions favoring a more optimistic conclusion.[2] At stake in these debates is whether Loney's death should be seen as the active choice of a contemporary warrior, or the tragic passing of a stereotypical "breed."

Critics who object to Loney's character, such as Louis Owens, go so far as to say that he is wholly "deracinated," deprived of any recognizably Indian qualities (150). Others, like John Purdy, discover the presence of distinct, if subtle, references to Gros Ventre practices in the novel, while Robert Nelson argues that in Welch's early works, including *Jim Loney*, identification with the Montana landscape takes place "independent of the mediation of any specific cultural tradition" but consistent with Indian tradition (95). With Nelson, I view aspects of Loney's character as consistent with specific dimensions of contemporary American Indian identity and agree that his distress does not signify "that Welch's creative vision concedes the *necessity* of alienation in the human condition" (94). To say that Loney's death, or his life, is devoid of Indian features is to discount the losses he suffers. In fact, *The Death of Jim Loney* offers a compelling portrait of one man's culturally specific response to a history of trauma. This is more readily apparent when we read the novel in the context of resemblances in grief patterns of the children of Jewish Holocaust survivors and those of some American Indians. Particularly useful to this interpretation is Ellen S. Fine's idea of an "absent memory," a feeling on the part of the children of survivors that their thoughts and emotions are dominated by the very memory they lack, of the Holocaust and the way of life it destroyed.

An effective model of cross-cultural work based on Holocaust theory is already under way in clinical settings dealing with American Indian populations. Clinicians such as Eduardo and Bonnie Duran and Maria Yellow Horse Brave Heart utilize Holocaust theory in their work, drawing from psychiatrists who confirm the impact of the Holocaust as a valid framework for comprehending "certain behavior patterns, symptoms, roles, and values" among members of the second generation (Danieli 9).[3] Acknowledging that the concept of intergenerational trauma has "long been known to healers and elders in Native American communities," they find similarities in grief patterns among Indians and the children of survivors, exhibited in behaviors not usually attributed to the effects of trauma ("Trauma of History" 60; "Soul Wound" 345). They identify relevant features of the theory in predominant life themes having to do with anxiety and guilt, including "a perceived obligation to share in ancestral pain as well as identification with the deceased ancestors," "compensatory fantasies," "unresolved grief," symptoms including nightmares, and extended "withdrawal and isolation" ("Soul Wound" 342). As Brave Heart demonstrates, familiarity with these themes helps to build a foundation from which to assist patients in uncovering unconsciously registered grief and performing crucial mourning processes (291–92).[4]

If ascribing symptomatic behaviors to the effects of trauma rather than to "deficiencies within the Native American community" combats "a form of epistemic violence that only exacerbates the problem," then viewing Loney's response to overwhelming loss as psychologically convincing from both an American Indian and a Western perspective helps to extricate his character from a discussion that tends to cast him as either heroic or tragic ("Trauma of History" 62). Anne Anlin Cheng writes that for members of racist societies, subjectivity is formed through a "convoluted, ongoing, generative and at times self-contradicting negotiation with pain" (15). Loney's death may be understood as the result of this kind of negotiation, evidence of his desire for an experience that he believes will connect him to his tribe and alleviate the suffering caused by his absent memory of the past. Understanding that Loney reacts to a history that is passed down to him, in the words of Henri Raczymow, "precisely as something not passed down" ("Memory" 103), we are able to view his death from a perspective that includes its potentially redemptive symbolic power within a traditional worldview as well as its origins in historically produced circumstances that encompass a history of trauma. We come to see him as more than "almost a parody of the Indian mixedblood as tragic victim caught between worlds," without minimizing the impact of the tremendous losses he has faced (Owens 156).

The possibility that Loney has inherited a legacy of trauma is difficult to dispute. As the Durans and Brave Heart write, "European contact decimated the indigenous populations of this hemisphere," through disease, alcohol, violence, and "policies systematically attacking the core of identity—language and the family system," including the creation of the boarding schools and the outlawing of religious practices ("Trauma of History" 62–64). The latter half of the nineteenth century brought the reservation system, the destruction of the buffalo herds, and the forced cession of land under the Allotment Act (Flannery 22–23; Brave Heart and DeBruyn 64). Like that of other Plains tribes, the history of the Gros Ventres was shaped by these events, the population decreasing sharply around the turn of the century following the setting of the boundaries of the Fort Belknap Reservation (Flannery 24). A period of "revitalization" followed, though after the Indian Reorganization Act the "reservation entered a period of steady decline" (Fowler 98–102). Loretta Fowler notes that the middle of the century, when Loney would have been growing up, was a time of "outright despair," for the Gros Ventres, as Termination Era policies led to economic hardship, a decrease in traditional practices, and an increase in migration away from the reservation (99–102).

Loney's existence is marked by the continuing effects of this history, an idea that is reinforced by his anticipation of the "cuts and bruises" that the young boy Amos After Buffalo will eventually suffer (166). He is cast about as a child, from the home of a social worker in Harlem to a mission school, where he is miserable, then back to Harlem, where he boards with a minister and graduates from high school along with several friends who will also die young. Yet while he senses that his "trouble" is rooted in the past, Loney has difficulty identifying it. He feels like an amnesiac but "without the amnesiac's clean slate," so that in thinking of his past, "all the people and events were as hopelessly tangled as a bird's nest in his mind" (20). When his white girlfriend, Rhea, asks what bothers him, he has difficulty answering: "It's not something . . . I don't even know myself. It has to do with the past. . . . It has to do with certain things. It has to do with my mother and father, but there are other things" (104). The traces, the hinted-at presence of things he cannot fix in words, are the source of Loney's anguish. His feeling of amnesia as well as his uneasy sense that something from the past is responsible for his unhappiness suggest their basis in the lingering presence of trauma that has been transmitted to him as absence.

Similar to the children of survivors, Loney is haunted by an "absent memory" of trauma, which will compel him to participate in an act of "originary trauma" in the form of his own death (Hartman 159). Fine writes that "absence, particularly the absence of memory, is a principal theme . . . of those writing in the aftermath" of the Holocaust (44). Memory is closed off from them not only because of their own belatedness but also because of the silences of the survivor generation. The absence of knowledge about the past increases its hold on those whose own experience can seem unimportant when compared to the horrific past they did not live through and will never know. In Fine's view, members of the second generation are plagued by

> the guilt of nonparticipation, a kind of regret for having been born too late. They are haunted by the world that has vanished; a large gap exists in their history, and they desire to bridge this gap, to be informed about what occurred, to know something about members of their family who perished. However, they feel frustrated by the impotence of incomprehension; the past eludes and excludes them. Repeatedly met with the silence of their parents and relatives—who transmit the wounds of genocide, and not the memory—they grow up in the "compact void of the unspeakable," as Nadine Fresco affirms. (43–44)

The absent memory of trauma is a dominant presence in their lives, their identity seemingly located in an unknowable event (46). Occasionally, they go so far as to seek out experiences resembling those endured by survivors in an attempt to relieve their own feelings of belatedness.[5]

The idea of an absent memory includes a number of themes in second-generation Holocaust theory that the clinicians identify as relevant to American Indian experience. Focusing on these themes in *Jim Loney*, as well as on the silences by which they are surrounded, allows us to arrive at an interpretation in which Loney's behavior remains mysterious and complex but that is also instructive in how trauma elicits behaviors among those who feel they have not experienced it directly. Fowler reports that many Gros Ventres had begun to return to the reservation by the 1960s, drawn by improved economic prospects and a renewed interest in ritual practices. Cultural resources are available to Loney, in the form of elders from whom he might seek guidance, as Nelson observes, or through members of his own generation, who in Fowler's account were highly active in reservation life by the late 1970s (Nelson 101; Fowler 1). Yet in portraying Loney's grief and isolation, Welch denies him access to these. Loney's immediate family offers little help in his effort to remember: his father, Ike, lives in Harlem but refuses to acknowledge Loney's existence, while his sister, Kate, lives in Washington, D.C., and maintains, "We have no past. What's the point in thinking about it?" (91). Instead, elusive signs suggest facets of Loney's absent memory, including his dreams and visions of his mother, the hinted-at presence of a living Indian culture and its associated spiritual realm on the nearby reservation, from which he feels excluded, and his vision of a dark bird, which he struggles to interpret.

His mother's absence is the sharpest reminder of Loney's personal devastation. As Owens writes, she "exists in some undefined place—maybe a madhouse, maybe death—just outside the picture," and her haunting presence appears in Loney's dreams and visions (149). What Loney eventually learns of her story hints at larger meanings in her disappearance, as it is after marrying a white man that she goes from participating in traditional dances and training as a nurse to dissolution and death. Loney fantasizes about their reunion, consistent with the "compensatory fantasies" described by the clinicians, and his unresolved grief for her is an important part of the emotional crisis that leaves him immobilized at his kitchen table.[6]

Loney's separation from his mother contributes to his feeling that he lacks an Indian identity. He is "startled" to find that "when he stepped out of his day-to-day existence he was considered an Indian" by other people; as for him, the "real" Indians are "the reservation families, all living under one roof, the old ones passing down the wisdom of their years, of their family's years, of their tribe's years, and the young ones soaking up their history, their places in history, with a wisdom that went beyond age" (102). Feeling cut off from the past in a way that resembles the sense of exile experienced by members of the second generation, Loney attributes an "authentic" Indian identity only to those who live according to his imagined ideal (Stromberg 48). In his reading of this passage, Ernest Stromberg observes that while Loney "recognizes the existence of contemporary Native American communities . . . that continue to engage in cultural performances which provide them with a sense of connection to a shared ancestry," he has difficulty feeling connected to them, as "the authenticity he attributes to these 'real' Indians eclipses the authenticity of his own identity" (48). Focused as he is on memory and the past, Loney understands Indian identity to be based on precisely those things he lacks. Rhea remarks that Loney is "lucky to have two sets of ancestors" so that he "can be Indian one day and white the next," but he does not experience his background as an opportunity to create a multiple or hybrid self (14). Instead, he struggles with it as a heavy burden of loss.

Experiencing his heritage as loss, from the time he is a child Loney finds many of the hints he receives about his past to be frightening, from the pictographs at Snake Butte to a passage from Isaiah that he repeatedly remembers.[7] Overwhelmed by his lack of memory but afraid of the answers to his questions, Loney experiences the unknown as ominous. Finally, when he shoots a childhood friend while on a hunting trip (an event that, like many others in the novel, is difficult to fully explain), he assumes the worst will happen to him as a result. Loney believes the shooting was prompted by the appearance of an "agent of evil," and afterward he is convinced that "it could only end badly" for him (129). Understanding his life story within an existing pattern of loss, Loney can only imagine an outcome ending in his death: "He knew he was marked, that it was a matter of time" (121).

Loney's assumption of his own guilt implies that along with an absent memory, he suffers from what Fine calls the "guilt of nonparticipation," worsened by his lack of a connection to a living, thriving community. After the accident, he feels that "somehow, at some time, everything had gone dreadfully wrong, and though it had something to do with his family, it had everything to do with himself" (134). Later, he confronts his father, in a fruitless attempt to gain knowledge about the past. Feeling "an old hatred stirring within him" as he begins his first conversation with Ike in fourteen years, by the end of their talk Loney no longer resents the older man for any wrongdoing. He assigns that guilt to himself instead: "Loney knew who the guilty party was. It was he who was guilty, and in a way that made his father's past sins seem childish, as though original sin were something akin to stealing candy bars" (146). His guilt contributes to his desire to participate in an incident similar to those that he imagines have preceded his birth: seeing himself as "marked" by his wrongdoing, he leaves his father's trailer prepared to be hunted down and killed.

Loney's final journey takes him onto the reservation and into the Little Rockies. Having left clues to his whereabouts for the police, he knows they will find him. Before he enters Mission Canyon, Loney thinks about "the Indians who had used the canyon, the hunting parties, the warriors, the women . . . he thought of the children who had played in the stream, and the lovers. These thoughts made him comfortable and he wasn't afraid" (168). Able for the first time to connect with a memory of his mother's people, Loney finds comfort, but it is only through inflicting violence directly upon himself. Loney's experience here seems more authentic to him than anything that has come before, as he reenacts a painful scene from American cultural narratives of Indians being destined to perish.

On a quest for the memory of a single event that will bring "order" to his life, Loney seeks to bring validity to his own experience. Yet for those born into the aftermath of violence, this can be difficult to achieve. Geoffrey Hartman writes that

> *the desire for experience, for being a contemporary witness of one's own life, fully present to it*, points to an expression satisfied only at an imagined horizon that merges sublimity and death. . . . Alternatively, that horizon as an origin, as a developmental event lodged deep in the past, compels a virtually endless effort to recover an originary trauma that must be brought into the space of conscious experience. Life, viewed this way, turns into a quest, centered on that defining but unconsciously experienced event. (159; italics in the original)

At the end of *Jim Loney*, Loney recreates what seems to be an originary trauma. He engages in what historian and trauma theorist Dominick LaCapra calls "acting out," a mode of dealing with trauma in which "the past is performatively regenerated or relived as if it were fully present" (716), rather than working through it, by engaging in the only kind of "cultural performance" he sees himself as being capable of, his death.

Earlier, when Loney is incapable of telling Rhea what troubles him, he instead tells her of the dark bird that appears in his visions. His description of the bird subtly replaces a description of his past. While the bird may indeed be a vision sent by his mother's people, as he suspects, unskilled as Loney is in tribal modes of understanding, its meaning always eludes him. It becomes a signifier that reveals nothing, an emblem of a past he cannot remember, both his own personal history and that of the Indian tribe to which he belongs. In this reading, the dark bird is the symbol of Loney's absent memory, the loss that is always present to him: his missing mother and his inability to consider himself an Indian, which has rendered his existence meaningless.[8] The absent memory that has haunted him throughout his life drives him to his own death, and the last things he sees before he dies are "the beating wings of a dark bird as it climbed to a distant place" (179). The dark bird leads Loney onward, but, like his memory, it seems forever out of his reach.

In considering how we might read *The Death of Jim Loney* in the light of cross-cultural theory, it is important to examine how the novel speaks back to that theory as well. In Holocaust discourse, metaphors of absence have been important to discussions of the crisis in representation said to have been precipitated by the event.[9] Recently, however, Debarati Sanyal has explored the theoretical function of absence within discussions of the transmission of trauma. She maintains that reading Holocaust texts for their "silences and aporias" can make trauma seem too easily transmitted and absorbed, diminishing "historical specificity" and rendering it "an ongoing metaphorical, cultural, and psychic condition that circulates from one subject—and history—to another" (16). Her concerns resemble those of critics such as Vizenor, who grow impatient with seemingly eternal narratives of Indian "victimry" (91). As a remedy, Sanyal recommends literature that obeys a "double injunction" to "situate oneself rigorously vis-à-vis the represented event while attending to its traumatic reverberations in our imagination," which will facilitate a more "ethical relationship to the past" (21).

Welch employs absence in keeping with these criteria, utilizing it to illuminate the specific causes of Loney's distress.[10] Throughout the novel, Welch seems to suggest that a history of the Gros Ventre people would provide the context for understanding the stark absences in the text. Loney's return to the reservation reveals that his story could not have taken place anywhere else; as Nelson argues, he forms a forceful identification with the land (95). Encouraged to leave Montana in order to escape everything from his visions to the police, believing that he has "lost forever the secret of survival," Loney is nevertheless rooted in the place and the seemingly elusive history that attaches there (155). In Loney's connection to the reservation, Welch exhibits the clearly situated viewpoint for which Sanyal advocates. Trauma is represented as a history transmitted as absence, without being presented as a transhistorical condition. The denials in the text are not presented as inevitable; Loney's death on the reservation is neither that of a victim nor of a hero. Rather, it is shown to be a culturally specific response to trauma, its meanings more readily available when viewed from a cross-cultural perspective. In asking us to bear witness to a death that is so difficult to explain, Welch keeps us looking for answers, deepening our relationship to the past and broadening the context in which we understand it.

NOTES

1. Comparisons between the genocide of the Jews and of the Native peoples of North America have been highly visible in the controversial work of Ward Churchill, who has characterized Holocaust scholarship that focuses on the uniqueness of the event as equivalent to a form of Holocaust denial (429). Other scholars, including historian David E. Stannard, have sought to draw from the iconic status of the Holocaust in comparing it to the devastation of Indians caused by European contact. A full review of the intersections between Holocaust studies and American Indian studies exceeds the scope of this essay. However, it is important to note, as Michael Rothberg writes in his illuminating discussion of the issue of uniqueness in genocide studies, that "An overly rigid focus on memory competition . . . distracts from other ways of thinking about the relation between histories and their memorial legacies" (1233). Less codified than the Holocaust in the cultural imagination, the concept of multigenerational trauma opens up promising directions for considering the intersections between the two fields.

2. Perspectives on Loney locate him on what Ernest Stromberg calls a "Native American literary continuum" (34). Paula Gunn Allen holds that Loney participates in a version of "vision-questing or 'crying for pity' as it is practiced on the Northern Plains" and that he "chooses a warrior's death" (91, 145). Several scholars see him as having what John Purdy calls an "almost instinctual" link to a range of Indian beliefs and practices, from Gros Ventre religion, as Purdy argues, to the land, as Robert Nelson claims, or to "the spirits of ancestors who have inhabited his confused visions in life," as Catherine

Rainwater suggests (106). They take Loney's willingness to give himself over to larger forces as evidence of his connection to his people. Finally, Louis Owens insists that "Loney enacts the fate of the epic Vanishing American" (155). The wide span of these convincing interpretations of the novel illustrates its power to provoke argument and debate.

3. The notion of a second generation depends upon the now widely accepted idea that the Holocaust can be a "core existential and relational experience for both generations," survivors and their children (Auerhahn and Laub 21). According to Efraim Sicher, "The second generation came to attention in case studies of Holocaust survivors' families in psychological literature from the 1970s, but they also began to identify as a group during the rise of ethnic consciousness and student activism in the United States" (397). Eva Hoffman credits the publication of Helen Epstein's volume *Children of the Holocaust: Conversations with Sons and Daughters of Survivors* in 1979 with heralding the arrival of the second generation of the Holocaust as a "recognized entity" (xi–xii).

4. Brave Heart primarily writes of her successful work with her own tribe, the Lakotas, but believes that her "model is universally relevant among native people" (300). She also recognizes that multigenerational trauma may be present in similar ways in other populations, including, for example, the children of those imprisoned in internment camps for Japanese Americans in the United States during World War Two (292).

5. Literature from England, the United States, Israel, and France offers a number of examples of members of the second generation who hurt themselves in a (sometimes unconscious) effort to gain insight into their parents' suffering. Works include, for example, *The War After: Living with the Holocaust*, by Anne Karpf, and *After Long Silence: A Memoir*, by Helen Fremont, memoirs in which the daughters of survivors manifest physical symptoms related to their parents' trauma, and the novel *See Under: Love*, by David Grossman, in which a young boy becomes consumed by his need to know the Nazi "beast." Similarly, Henri Raczymow's novel *Writing the Book of Esther* describes how Esther, born in France near the end of the war and named for an aunt who perished in the camps, dons prisoners' garb, starves herself, and ultimately commits suicide in response to the overwhelming psychic burden of events she did not experience directly.

6. In "Momaday, Welch, and Silko: Expressing the Feminine Principle through Male Alienation," Judith A. Antell suggests that all three authors "separate" their protagonists "from Indian women and the feminine principle," a device that underscores the characters' loneliness and isolation (217).

7. The passage reads: "Turn away from man in whose nostrils is breath, for of what account is he?" (1). For a discussion of its relevance to the novel, see Rainwater, *Dreams of Fiery Stars*.

8. Rainwater notes that, near the end of the book, "the narrator equates this 'dark bird' with the memories that Jim cannot piece together into his own story" (150). My own reading resembles this view but emphasizes the bird's function in representing Loney's absent memory, versus memories of his own experiences.

9. Georgio Agamben urges us "to listen to what is unsaid" in survivor testimony, for example, in order to discover the presence of that which defies description, while psychiatrist Nadine Fresco recounts that her second-generation patients experience the losses of the Holocaust as a "phantom pain," akin to having "had a hand amputated that they never had" (Agamben 14; Fresco 421).

10. Several critics compare Welch to western authors who employ gaps or absences in their writing. In his analysis of *Winter in the Blood*, Paul Eisenstein finds strong similarities between Welch and Ernest Hemingway, citing their shared use of "omitted history" to signify, respectively, an unknown tribal history, and the impact of World War One (2). Nelson points to resemblances between Loney's killing of Pretty Weasel and the murder of the Arab by Meursault in Albert Camus's *The Stranger* but insists that by having Loney find meaning in what might seem to be an absurd event Welch shifts our interpretation away from an existentialist model (120).

WORKS CITED

Agamben, Georgio. *Remnants of Auschwitz: The Witness and the Archive*. Trans. Daniel Heller-Roazen. New York: Zone Books, 1999.

Allen, Paula Gunn. *The Sacred Hoop: Recovering the Feminine in American Indian Traditions*. Boston: Beacon P, 1992.

Antell, Judith A. "Momaday, Welch, and Silko: Expressing the Feminine Principle through Male Alienation." *American Indian Quarterly* 12.3 (1998): 213–20.

Auerhahn, Nanette C., and Dori Laub. "Intergenerational Memory of the Holocaust." Danieli, *International Handbook*, 21–41.

Brave Heart, Maria Yellow Horse. "The Return to Sacred Path: Healing the Historical Trauma and Historical Unresolved Grief Response among the Lakota through a Psychoeducational Group Intervention." *Smith College Studies in Social Work* 68.3 (1998): 288–305.

Brave Heart, Maria Yellow Horse, and Lemyra M. DeBruyn. "The American Indian Holocaust: Healing Historical Unresolved Grief." *American Indian and Alaska Native Mental Health Research* 8.2 (1998): 60–82.

Cheng, Anne Anlin. *The Melancholy of Race: Psychoanalysis, Assimilation, and Hidden Grief.* New York: Oxford UP, 2001.

Churchill, Ward. *A Little Matter of Genocide: Holocaust and Denial in the Americas, 1492 to the Present.* San Francisco: City Lights Books, 1997.

Danieli, Yael, ed. *International Handbook of Multigenerational Legacies of Trauma. The Plenum Series on Stress and Coping*, ed. Yael Danieli. New York: Plenum P, 1998.

Danieli, Yael. Introduction. Danieli, *International Handbook*, 1–17.

Duran, Bonnie, Eduardo Duran, and Maria Yellow Horse Brave Heart. "Native Americans and the Trauma of History." *Studying Native America: Problems and Prospects.* Ed. Russell Thornton. Madison: U of Wisconsin P, 1998. 60–76.

Duran, Eduardo, Bonnie Duran, Maria Yellow Horse Brave Heart, and Susan Yellow Horse-Davis. "Healing the American Indian Soul Wound." Danieli, *International Handbook*, 341–54.

Eisenstein, Paul. "Finding Lost Generations: Recovering Omitted History in *Winter in the Blood.*" *MELUS* 19.3 (1994): 3–19.

Fine, Ellen S. "The Absent Memory: The Act of Writing in Post-Holocaust French Literature." *Writing and the Holocaust.* Ed. Berel Lang. New York: Holmes and Meier, 1988. 41–57.

Flannery, Regina. *The Gros Ventre of Montana, Part I: Social Life.* Washington, D.C.: Catholic U of America P, 1953.

Fowler, Loretta. *Shared Symbols, Contested Meanings: Gros Ventre Culture and History, 1778–1984.* Ithaca: Cornell UP, 1987.

Fremont, Helen. *After Long Silence: A Memoir.* New York: Dell/Random House, 1999.

Fresco, Nadine. "Remembering the Unknown." *International Review of Psycho-Analysis* 11 (1984): 417–27.

Grossman, David. *See Under: Love.* Trans. Betsy Rosenberg. New York: Noonday Press-Farrar, Straus and Giroux, 1989.

Hartman, Geoffrey H. *The Longest Shadow: In the Aftermath of the Holocaust.* Bloomington: Indiana UP, 1996.

Hoffman, Eva. *After Such Knowledge: Memory, History, and the Legacy of the Holocaust.* New York: Public Affairs-Perseus Books Group, 2004.

Karpf, Anne. *The War After: Living with the Holocaust.* London: Minerva, 1997.

LaCapra, Dominick. "Trauma, Absence, Loss." *Critical Inquiry* 25 (Summer 1999): 696–727.

Momaday, N. Scott. *House Made of Dawn*. New York: Perennial Library-Harper and Row, 1968.

Nelson, Robert M. *Place and Vision: The Function of Landscape in Native American Fiction. American Indian Studies 1*. New York: Peter Lang, 1992.

Owens, Louis. *Other Destinies: Understanding the American Indian Novel. American Indian Literature and Critical Studies*. Norman: U of Oklahoma P, 1992.

Purdy, John. "Bha'a and *The Death of Jim Loney*." *SAIL* 5.2 (1993): 67–71.

Rainwater, Catherine. *Dreams of Fiery Stars: The Transformations of Native American Fiction*. Philadelphia: U of Pennsylvania P, 1999.

Raczymow, Henri. "Memory Shot through with Holes." *Yale French Studies* 85 (1994): 98–105.

———. *Writing the Book of Esther*. Trans. Dori Katz. New York: Holmes and Meier, 1995.

Rothberg, Michael. "The Work of Testimony in the Age of Decolonization: *Chronicle of a Summer*, Cinema Verité, and the Emergence of the Holocaust Survivor." *PMLA* 119.5 (2004): 1231–46.

Sanyal, Debarati. "A Soccer Match in Auschwitz: Passing Culpability in Holocaust Criticism." *Representations* 79 (Summer 2002): 1–27.

Sicher, Eraim. "The 'Second-Generation' Holocaust Novel." *Holocaust Novelists*. Ed. Eraim Sicher. *Dictionary of Literary Biography* 299. Detroit: Gale, 2004. 397–407.

Silko, Leslie Marmon. *Ceremony*. New York: Penguin Books, 1986.

Stannard, David E. *American Holocaust: Columbus and the Conquest of the New World*. New York: Oxford UP, 1992.

Stromberg, Ernest. "The Only Real Indian Is a Dead Indian: The Desire for Authenticity in James Welch's *The Death of Jim Loney*." *SAIL* 10.4 (1998): 33–53.

Vizenor, Gerald. *Fugitive Poses: Native American Scenes of Absence and Presence. The Abraham Lincoln Lecture Series*. Lincoln: U of Nebraska P, 1998.

Welch, James. *The Death of Jim Loney*. New York: Penguin, 1979.

———. *Winter in the Blood*. New York: Penguin, 1974.

"There Is a Right Way"

PHILLIP H. ROUND
University of Iowa

James Welch's *Riding the Earthboy 40* remains a watershed work in American poetry more than thirty years after its initial publication in 1971. Some would argue it has maintained its prominence because it accomplishes an historically and materially genuine confessional regionalism that Welch's mentor at the University of Montana, Richard Hugo, professed but never quite achieved. Others would say that Welch's book remains vital because it initiated a new era in Native American poetry. There were other important works by Native poets prior to *Riding the Earthboy 40*—significant poems by N. Scott Momaday and Duane Niatum—but none collected into a single book with the intercultural impact of Welch's compilation.[1]

On the jacket of the 2004 Penguin edition, Sherman Alexie calls *Riding the Earthboy 40* "one of my true holy bibles." Joy Harjo cites it as "a touchstone for a generation who were figuring out a poetry that had to be assembled from broken treaties, stolen lands, the blues, horses, fast cars, and long rough nights." I would like to explore why this collection of lyric poetry, published by a writer who would become much more famous for his novels, remains so influential, both within American Indian literary circles and among a broader group of readers and writers who consider it an essential part of the larger American literary canon.

Riding the Earthboy 40 enjoys this range of effect, I believe, because James Welch turned his early and amazing grasp of the Euramerican lyric to the real-world ethical questions that engaged him as a young American Indian man in 1960s Montana. His collection remains powerful because Welch never gave an inch as either a craftsman or a human being. Through Euramerican lyric practice, he gave formal expression to his feelings in ways that never compromised their anger or their plaintiveness. If traditional lyrical poetry in English was born of the "enemy's language," *Riding the Earthboy 40* reclaimed it as a viable expressive mode for a generation of Native Americans who were coming of age in those tumultuous years just prior to the occupations of Alcatraz and Wounded Knee. A close reading of one of the collection's most economical and highly crafted lyrics, "There Is a Right Way," demonstrates the process by which Welch harnessed the lyric form to his own emerging historical consciousness—what he calls his "renegade words"—as a Blackfeet/Gros Ventre man taking stock of his life at the middle of the twentieth century.

Although Welch's collection as a whole is both stylistically and politically challenging, "There Is a Right Way" is in many ways conventional. It is a lyric that meditates on a specific occasion and whose form models the speaker's transforming consciousness as he engages in contemplation. Yet Welch's poem is at once exemplary of the convention and exceeds it, locating his speaker in a windy Montana landscape, where he witnesses a prairie hawk's pursuit of a field mouse. In subject and occasion, Welch's lyric finds analogs in works like Robert Frost's "Design" and Elizabeth Bishop's "The Fish." But where Frost's experience of the predator-prey relationship leads him to muse on the Christian argument of design, "There Is a Right Way" explores the "justice" of the scene and the way that it forces the speaker to abandon conventional ethical or moral considerations. In the end, the reader is also left to ponder rightness and justice from a perspective outside the conventional Euramerican discourses of morality and justice.

Welch's meditation immediately strikes out in this startling direction by tuning its simple diction to an unexpected discursive field. It is the "justice" of the prairie hawk's actions that moves the speaker to contemplation. The reader is thus instantly implicated in an ethical situation, even before the poem's occasion completely reveals itself. The word "justice" also creates suspense. What hangs in the balance? Is the following scene somehow related to the discourse of jurisprudence, that institutional script of the many-centuries-long fight of Indian peoples for sovereignty?

Welch enhances the opening line's semantic suspense and intertextuality by masterfully pitting enjambment against medial caesura to offer the reader an almost kinesthetic analog for how this scene "moved" him. Fitting breathless wonder to manifest rightness, the speaker reports that

> the justice of the prairie hawk
> moved me; his wings tipped
> the wind just right. (48)

The internal echoing, if not rhyming, of "justice" and "just" underscore the poem's ethical meditation at the level of sentence sound, shifting the root word's meaning again, this time from the juridical to the personal and colloquial.

In fact, the poem's delicate ethical balance is sustained by the verb "tipped"—the prairie hawk's hunt is certainly aided by the wind but only in a relational way. Neither wings nor air alone seem capable of capturing the elusive prey. Welch further emphasizes the scene's unconventional morality by asserting that "the mouse / was any mouse." Semantically equivalent, the two signifiers are further drained of difference through enjambment.

It is at this moment that the poet's employs medial caesura to enforce a lyric "turn," moving from setting the scene of the poem's occasion to suggesting that occasion's effect on the speaker's consciousness:

> I came away,
> broken from my standing spot,
> dizzy with the sense of a world
> trying to be right.(48)

Again, Welch's verbs—though simple and straightforward, like all of the diction in the poem—suspend moral judgment, suggesting a justice that is both relational and unexpected. Once "broken" from his ethical stasis, the speaker senses that the surrounding universe is at least "trying" to be right.

Therein lies the poem's great ethical achievement—to appreciate the world's tendency toward the good, the graceful, and the forgiving. This is quintessential James Welch, and understanding this point of view is key to appreciating characters like Jim Loney and the unnamed narrator of *Winter in the Blood*. To be like the protagonist of Welch's first novel, to find oneself as distant from one's inner self "as a hawk from the moon," (*Winter* 2) is often a given in Indian Country. But to find in this "event of distance" (*Winter* 161) an imperative to act in a "right way," that is the poet's quest.

Yet Welch's lyric does not stop there. "There Is a Right Way" concludes with a line and half of concrete nouns in a series that once again takes the potentially abstract sense of ethical justice achieved in the previous lines and submits it to the trial of the landscape of real things. The world is trying to be right, and the mouse is "a part of a wind that stirs the plains." By "breaking" the reader from "the standing spot" of apostrophic self-consciousness (and overt moralizing) on the part of the speaker, Welch forces us to relinquish metaphorical responses in favor or metonymical ones. Mouse, wind, and plains become parts of a larger whole, but this whole has nothing like Frost's "design" directing it. Rather, the lone verb here—"stirs"—suggests a nonlinear, circular motion as the "shape" that moral rightness takes in the world being witnessed. By leaving this final revelation to the reader, not the speaker, Welch formally opens the lyric to the landscape itself, releasing the speaker's own consciousness to the outside world.

This final gesture, in turn, invites us to revisit the poem's title. There is a right way, and it is indeed a "way" or direction, not a unitary divinity or prescriptive set of laws. "Getting Things Straight," as the title of the poem that follows in the collection suggests, is to be found in the process, rather than the solution, of moral or ethical questioning.

This ethical realization is also central to the poetical practice of the book as a whole, and to its sustained importance to American literature. By pulling back from a close reading of "There Is a Right Way," one can see its relation to the careful way James Welch constructed the whole collection. *Riding the Earthboy 40* is divided into four sections—"Knives," "The Renegade Wants Words," "Day after Chasing Porcupines," and "The Day the Children Took Over."[2] The third section, in which "There Is a Right Way" appears, is organized around meditations on the same set of images that are found in the poem—field mice, preying hawks, and a windy rural landscape.

The section "Day after Chasing Porcupines" comes after two sections of verse that dramatize Welch's amazing poetic range. The first employs Latin American surrealist techniques along the lines of Cesar Vallejo to engage the violence of Native American dispossession and the deep social and psychological knife wounds that still fester in many American Indian peoples and communities.[3] "The Renegade Wants Words" follows this difficult, image-driven set of poems with an equally powerful critique of contemporary Indian-white relations and Native life that is deeply indebted to colloquial rhythms, Native naming, and careful line and stanza division. Perhaps the most famous poem from this section, "Christmas Comes to Moccasin Flat" epitomizes the way Welch harnesses lyric practice to local sounds and knowledge:

> Christmas comes like this: Wise men
> unhurried, candles bought on credit (poor price
> for calves), warriors face down in wine sleep. (22)

"Day after Chasing Porcupines" is a quiet section by comparison, and its title poem finds an old mongrel dog sleeping a fitful sleep beneath a farm shed while nursing a muzzle full of porcupine quills. Around him is a familiar landscape. "Hawks / glittered through the morning clouds," while "Timid chickens watched chickens in puddles" (41). As in "There Is a Right Way," the moment hangs suspended. The hawk doesn't get the chickens; the mongrel continues to sleep, as "wind ruffled his mongrel tail, / the lazy cattails and the rain." Again, the wind "stirs" the scene in a *right* way but without a conventional ethical direction. Even the next poem, "Surviving," with its chilling image of near-starvation in Indian Country, suspends the poem's central action—when "wet black things . . . sneak away our cache / or meat"—in a final ellipsis: "To stay alive this way, it's hard. . . ." (42).

"Surviving" is followed by "Snow Country Weavers," an epistolary lyric that reports the speaker's well-being as though to a distant correspondent. The predators here are wolves, but they are dying at the speaker's door, as the harsh winter wind "drives them from their meat" (43). Saved from death—"surviving," once again—the speaker has a vision of spiders weaving webs "filled with words / that tumbled meaning into wind" (43). As in many of this section's lyrics, there is a tension between the "tumbling," almost random, direction of the wind and the tight quatrains that make up the poem. The organization of the poem mirrors that of the spider webs, as diction and imagery roll out to break free from the tight skein of the poem's formal elements. "Surviving" is followed soon after by "Birth on Range 18," another poem from "Day after Chasing Porcupines" that fuses a rigorous stanza pattern (this time couplets) to a scene of survival and a moment of revelation. As a calf is born, the mother's eyes catch the speaker's "stare" and force him to break his gaze. His gaze "broken," the speaker finds that

> Moon eclipsed the night. We rode the wind
>
> the only distance we could muster—
> quick paces and a space of mind. (46)

The section's last three poems—"There Is a Right Way," "Getting Things Straight," and "The Versatile Historian"—build on this repetition of imagery and poetic practices to portray successive stages in the speaker's quest for a spiritual vision on the plains. After leaving the scene of the circling prairie hawk, the speaker plunges into doubt and questioning. "Getting Things Straight" asks, "The hawk—is he still rising, circling . . . ?" "What does it mean?" "Is he my vision?" (49). If "Day after Chasing Porcupines" offers an answer to these doubts, that answer is most fully crafted in "The Versatile Historian," the section's concluding poem. This lyric is, in fact, the "key" to the whole group of poems in the section, but it too suspends overt moral or ethical imperative in favor of craft and process. Again, Welch uses imagery shared throughout the poems of this section—wind, broad sky, clouds—but to different effect. It seems as though the speaker is much deeper into his vision quest at this point and has formed almost a sense of vocation, of a job to do. He will become an historian, yet the kind of history he will produce will be like no other in the Euramerican tradition. It will arise from song, its "real words" having been robbed by sleeping weasels. As the poem builds to its climactic resolution of the speaker's uncertainty, the whole landscape begins to beat the time of the song the speaker will take as his own. "Chanting clouds" pulse above him, and "Everywhere, rhythm raged." The speaker even becomes unmoored from the sacred directions, as he find "the Sun beneath" his feet (50). He becomes a "statue"—an image both of the ethical stasis he has experience in other poems from this section and of the traditional kind of history is leaving behind. In this state he finds himself "needing friends," and the lyric employs the same tension between imagery and formal structures that has shaped so many of the verses in "Day after Chasing Porcupines." The speaker leaves us "needing friends in wind / that needed fire, mountains to bang against" (50). As in "There Is a Right Way," this speaker cannot break his ethical paralysis without connecting to the whole pulsating world. Like the mouse and the prairie hawk, this fire of transformation needs wind to breathe, and wind, in turn, needs mountains for its drum.

Read from within a now highly developed Native literary critical discourse, James Welch's lyric poetry in "Day after Chasing Porcupines" emerges as an example of what Gerald Vizenor has called "natural reason," an orientation toward both the natural world and the literature of dominance that "teases the sense that nature is precarious" (15). For Vizenor, natural reason operates as an ethical imperative within a contemporary American Indian literature of survivance, poised against a Euramerican field of domination in which "chance and fate" are denied Native peoples, replaced by stasis, stagnation, and nostalgia. Welch's lyric voice, a voice that wrests itself free time and again in *Riding the Earthboy 40*, is a voice schooled by a natural reason born of life on an Indian reservation. It represents Welch's earliest gesture toward a tribal ethic that has harnessed that most ineffable of the modes of the literature of dominance to its own raging rhythms and dizzying perspectives.

NOTES

1. Kenneth Lincoln locates the "Native American Renaissance" in poetry during the mid-1970s, when significant collections of American Indian verse

like *Come to Power* (1974), *Voices From Wah'kon-Tah* (1974), and *Carriers of the Dream Wheel* (1975) first appeared. These compilations were the first, Lincoln argues, where Indian poets from around the country "risked the personal voice, . . . showed the heart's pain, the bitter dust of past and present betrayal" (66). Duane Niatum edited *Carriers of the Dream Wheel* to include the poetry of seven Native American women and nine Native men whose average age was thirty-one and who presented readers with "a new Indian image of the educated traditionalist" (Lincoln 69). Niatum's own first collection of poetry, *Taos Pueblo*, was not published by Greenfield Review Press until a year after *Riding the Earthboy 40*, and Momaday's *Angle of Geese* (1974) and *Gourd Dancer* (1976) did not appear until several years later.

2. The 2004 Penguin edition prints the revised text of *Riding Earthboy 40* as it appeared in 1976. The collation of *Riding Earthboy 40* that Welch first produced in 1971 did not stress these divisions or share the later edition's careful arrangement.

3. Readers interested in Welch's use of Latin American symbolism may wish to consult Alan Velie's "James Welch's Poetry."

WORKS CITED

Lincoln, Kenneth. *Native American Renaissance*. U of California P, 1983.

Ruoff, A. LaVonne Brown. *American Indian Literatures: An Introduction, Bibliographic Review, and Selected Bibliography*. MLA, 1990.

Velie, Alan. "James Welch's Poetry." *American Indian Culture and Research Journal* 3.1 (1979): 19–38.

Vizenor, Gerald. *Manifest Manners: Postindian Warriors of Survivance*. Wesleyan, 1994.

Welch, James. *Riding the Earthboy 40*. 1971. Reprint, Penguin, 2004.

———. *Winter in the Blood*. 1974. Reprint, Penguin, 1986.

Closure in James Welch's *Fools Crow*

BETTE WEIDMAN
Queens College

In her study of Asian American cultural politics, *Immigrant Acts*, Lisa Lowe reminds us that the cultural institution of the novel performs a function in reconciling readers to the national social order. She points to the interruption of the novel form by immigrant writers, whose works "displace the representational regimes of the institutionalized novel and official historical narrative by writing out of the limits and breakdowns of those regimes" (101). Her analysis is helpful in understanding the elongated closure of James Welch's *Fools Crow* and in addressing his legacy to writers and readers. As critics have long noted, Welch displaces the familiar "western" and the official historical narratives of the victory of the civilized over the savage.[1] He constructs the story of Indian-white contact from inside Indian subjectivity and redefines the meanings of religion, culture, and virtue for a diverse audience.

With *Fools Crow*, Welch has produced a bildungsroman, which Lowe calls "the primary form for narrating the development of the individual from youthful innocence to civilized maturity." This form, she points out,

> has a special status among the works selected for a canon, for it elicits the reader's identification with the bildung narrative of ethical formation, itself a narrative of the individual's relinquishing of particularity and difference through identification with an idealized "national" form of subjectivity. (98)

If we see Welch as analogous to Lowe's interrupting immigrant writers, we have to ask to what national order does he seek to reconcile his subject? Who does he conceive to be his audience, and how does he shape his material to engage the identification of each cohort of a diverse readership? Does his novel belong exclusively to a subcanon of Native American literature, or does it seek to insert itself into a national canon, helping us to reframe the meaning of citizenship in the contemporary United States?

It is my contention that Welch enters both the subcanon of Native American novels and the U.S. national canon, that his novel explores the gap between official national histories, earlier canonized novels by Euramericans, and the hitherto only partially expressed point of view of Native Americans on the history of their conflict with the colonizers. There is a Pikuni social order to which Fools Crow is reconciled and that is universalized in the world of the novel. The encroaching social system of the whites is seen as other, as incoherent or corrupt.[2] Just as, in Lowe's argument, the reader of Jane Austen identified with Elizabeth Bennett even if he was reading in colonized Jamaica, so the reader of James Welch is forced by the novel form to affiliate with the subjectivity of White Man's Dog, later Fools Crow. Welch makes this inevitable by developing a series of reflectors for his hero: his friend Fast Horse, his brother Running Fisher, his opposite, Owl Child. The narrative distinguishes Fools Crow from his foils by showing his choices as in line with Pikuni ethics. Moreover, the novel specifies band names, a level of accuracy not hitherto found in American novels. Names for the characters and their naming practices also enter the novel in substantial detail.

Welch sets his novel just at the moment at which Pikuni social order is under maximum stress, a period all readers know was followed by calamity: military defeat, epidemic, starvation. Yet for the first time in an American novel, the reader sees a broad picture of nineteenth-century Native-Euramerican conflict from within the Native subjectivity.[3] Readers absorb the Blackfeet experience of encroachment on their lands, participate in their leadership's counseling, walk with Fools Crow through the massacred camp. On another level, riskier for the author, they listen to Fools Crow's conversations with Raven, experience the Sun Dance sacrifice with him, follow him into apprenticeship to the healer, and listen to the recalled stories of the Beaver Bundle and the fire-bearer. I call these narrative elements risky for Welch because, although the novel form can incorporate them, they represent a bold challenge to its conventional realism.

It is to the shared concept of the dream (shared, if understood differently in Native and in Euramerican cultures) that Welch owes the narrative integrity of his work. In spite of the different cultural positions of his diverse readership, all understand the deep interiority of the dream. Its admission into the narrative is the reader's fullest introduction to the framework of Pikuni psychology and social order. In recognizing the significance of the dreaming, diverse readers acknowledge their common humanity with Fools Crow. When, in a dream vision, he sees the future calamity of his people, he shares the reader's knowledge too; we come even closer to him. The dream vision is motivated by his bewilderment: what choices to make in a narrowing spectrum of possibilities. Imagined as the best mind and body his people could produce, ultimately he realizes that their only viable path is that of faithfulness to one other and to their communal values. Endurance in the service of the community as modeled in the Sun Dance sacrifice is the answer that awaits him and that he returns from the dream to live out.

Within the framework of a Pikuni social order, the novel offers a resolution to social and moral predicaments. Such a resolution speaks to the reading subject's present needs, to the descendents of the Pikunis, and by extension to other Native American groups searching for a meaningful relation to heritage. It also speaks to non-Native reading subjects who learn to resituate themselves in relation to nineteenth-century American history. Having been imaginatively placed in the position of a Pikuni for the duration of the text, the non-Native reader loses her exteriority and sees the application of Fools Crow's resolution to a variety of historical situations.

Readers interested in James Welch's legacy must see it, then, in the way he achieves closure in *Fools Crow*. Not just an end, optimistic or pessimistic, to his bildungs novel, he arrives at a closure that implies a new national social order: one that redefines current American values to include Blackfeet ethics and adds to the store of collective memory the stories of Seco-co-muckon, the Beaver hero Akaiyan and, above all, Feather Woman. All of Welch's readers, whether Native or non-Native, possess at the end a refreshed idea of the meaning of adulthood, of fidelity, of endurance through the inevitability of change. Equally, they recognize the ignorance, wastefulness, and brutality of the colonizer so well symbolized in the figure of the white hunter who leaves his kills. These unsparing meanings are modulated by scenes that the chapter structure and omniscient narration of the novel permit: the sympathetically told story of the Confederate deserter and the visit of Sturgis, the white doctor who urges smallpox inoculation.

Nora Barry, in "A Myth to Be Alive," claims that Welch has written a modern survival myth for the children of the Blackfeet and by extension other Native American groups decimated over centuries of genocide (3–20). But the postcolonial approach to the bildungsroman lets us see that Welch has written a survival myth for all of us. The ending is not a false optimism or a momentary stopgap but an affirmation of continuance and renewal of resources and energy. That this renewal is symbolized by the Blackfeet image of plenty—the return of spring rains and the buffalo herds—is a tribute to the symbols of that culture.

In contrast, Alan Velie thinks the novel is a romance and that the ending inspires nostalgia for a lost way of life (391–405). But nostalgia is not fostered in the reader by Welch's representation of Blackfeet life. He shows us a hard life, marked by warfare and violent death. Think of Mikapi's loss of his young wife, Yellow Kidney's mutilation and despair, and the way Kills Close to the Lake is made the property of a rich, older man and the slave of his wives.[4] Welch certainly implied that it was not a static culture but one that had evolved and would go on evolving. Some evidence of this is embedded in the scene in which Rides at the Door conceals his knowledge of English.

As readers make their way into Book Four, they are all struck by the audacity of the novelist, who takes the risk of introducing a journey into the myth world into his realistic historical novel. It is not a short journey either, as it structures the remainder of Book Four, in six chapters alternating dream journey with events in the everyday world. The myth of Feather Woman is not simply retold here, as it had been in Book One in the narrative surrounding Heavy Shield Woman's sponsorship of a Sun Dance, but it is reimagined as part of the quest undertaken by Fools Crow to relieve his quandary concerning the future of the Pikunis, which continues to unfold as he travels mythward.

There has been a great deal of critical writing about this narrative strategy and the contribution it makes to an understanding of the novelist's final position. Readings include the romantic (Velie), the ethnographic (Barry), the revision of the western (Chester), the employment of images from film (Shanley), the postcolonial (Scheckter), the post-Indian (Nelson), the magico-realist (Gish). Each reading has something to offer, but none points to the elegant simplicity with which the novel divides into two streams of narrative, one following Fools Crow into a world that is increasingly unfamiliar to him and finally through a narrow tunnel into another season.

Meanwhile, the novel's other characters remain, in the alternating chapters, on familiar ground, struggling with their unfolding plot lines: the return of Yellow Kidney's body, the confrontation of Rides at the Door and his son and third wife. Welch makes the myth world accessible by constructing a narrative bridge to it, using the archetypes of journey and dream shared by Pikunis and Euramericans, taking advantage of the very useful chapter divisions bequeathed him by the traditional novel. The rhythm of alternating chapters maintains the realism of the novel, for we all know that while we are away in dream or travel our families and home places continue to function without us.[5] Fools Crow is awake and aware of his body, moving through a physical world, yet he arrives at last in a place in imagination, a place whose meaning becomes clear to him as he realizes his need for guidance.

He is not in the Sky World with the Sun Father and Morning Star but in a Blackfeet version of purgatory. Feather Woman, a human being who has married a star but through loneliness has lost her place, lives on in a condition of mourning, gifted with immortality and foreknowledge but unable to regain her status as wife. This figure and the story of which she is a part belong to Blackfeet mythology. Christopher Nelson, in his book-length dissertation criticizing what he calls "ethnographic criticism," would have us read Feather Woman as a negative model for Fools Crow, one whose world must be rejected because it represents endless mourning. But Welch does not mix up his mythic figure and his human characters; Fools Crow and the reader respect the immutable mythic role of the woman with whom he exchanges an affectionate human touch. Welch emphasizes her role as an intercessor for suffering humanity. She is a little like the Virgin Mary in her relationship to divine power, a part of it, yet irremediably human and so more accessible to the questing Fools Crow than the powerful deities.

She is a figure born of the collective Blackfeet imagination drawn on by the novelist for a special role in his effort to retell the story of his people's confrontation with colonialist power. The way Welch imagines the transfer of Feather Woman's knowledge to Fools Crow is particularly striking. She paints on a yellow skin, an act that belongs to Pikuni culture, but when Fools Crow tries to see the painting, he perceives instead a moving picture, a film version of the future, where every detail of the coming catastrophe moves before him. The novelist gives the gift of modern cinematography to the traditional figure, along with her unsentimental vision. Surprisingly, Kathryn Shanley, in her short essay on *Fools Crow*, finds images out of western cinema—images she calls Indian kitsch—in the novel but does not mention the evocation of film at this critical juncture (131–38).

The ending of the novel is doubled; while it unsparingly tells the catastrophic story of the end of a way of life, it also shows that way as generating the psychological flexibility to continue. In one sense the story ends when Fools Crow reaches the goal of his vision quest and sees the future. However, Welch does not leave his exemplary character in possession of knowledge in that other world but brings him back to his present reality to face new birth, spring rains, and practices that celebrate cultural renewal.

It is at the end that we feel most aware of the subtle enlargement of Fools Crow's character from that of an individual Pikuni to an embodiment of the best qualities of his people. The procession, a rich device with a long history in religion and in American literature, lifts the characters into symbolic figures and frames their activity on the timeless space of ritual. Thus the novel transforms the carefully drawn particularity of historical circumstances, the demands of a complex religious belief, and the expression of a developed culture into a broad evocation of the best qualities of humanity in all times and places.

NOTES

1. From the early nineteenth-century works of James Fenimore Cooper to the twentieth-century novels of western writers like Zane Grey, Louis L'Amour and others, Euramerican writers have told the story of colonial displacement of Native Americans from the white point of view. Their representations of Indians as stereotyped nobles or savages succeeded in obscuring the realities of the genocide perpetrated by the U.S. government and its citizenry. Exceptions may be made for a few Euramerican writers who objected to the falsification and sought to know more. Henry David Thoreau is a good antidote to Cooper, Mari Sandoz a more satisfying writer on Native American subjects than her better-known twentieth-century contemporaries.

2. A good example is the account of the arrival of the "seizers" with Joe Kipp (153–58).

3. Blackfeet myth and religious belief play a central role in constructing as a story of events that befell the people in the late nineteenth century. Belief and ritual observance have explanatory and motivating importance in character development and in plot outcome. At critical junctures in the novel, specific figures of myth—Akaiyan, Feather Woman, Poia, Raven—are brought into harmony with historical realism. Novelistic action is generated by dream and vision quest; turning points, including one of closure, are marked by rituals of curing and celebration. In fact, the implication of the novel's structure is that understanding of the dynamic quality of the Blackfeet worldview is what makes sense of history. With the novel itself thus taking us behind surface historical events to deep structures of belief, we as readers are driven to look into Welch's sources and to examine his use of them. This is not to make the novel into ethnography: quite the opposite, it is to see that Welch regarded Blackfeet beliefs as viable interpretive strategies for living, powerful enough to reshape a foreign art form. Blackfeet belief renders the story tellable. It reminds the reader that storytelling is the common home of myth, religious belief, and the print-medium novel. A next step in research should involve a review of Welch's use of sources and a study of well-known bodies of recorded material, such as those by George Bird Grinnell, Walter McClintock, Clark Wissler, D.C. Duvall, Darnell Davis Rides at the Door, and others. The reader will also be reminded of the classic account of dream vision as an expression of belief

system in *Black Elk Speaks*, edited by John Neihardt, originally published in New York by William Morrow in 1932 and presently in print in a new edition (2000) from the University of Nebraska Press.

4. For Mikapi's wife, see Welch, 247–48; for Yellow Kidney, see Welch, 71–83; for Kills Close to the Lake, see Welch, 220–24, 340–43.

5. Chapters 29, 31, and 33 take place in the dream-vision world, while chapters 30, 32, and 34 take place in the everyday world.

WORKS CONSULTED

Bak, Hans. "The Art of Hybridization: James Welch's Fools Crow," *American Studies in Scandinavia* 27.1 (1995): 33–47.

Barry, Nora. "A Myth to Be Alive: James Welch's Fools Crow," *MELUS* 17.1 (1991): 3–20.

Chester, Blanca. "Western Fictions in Welch's *Fools Crow*." *Telling the Stories: Essays on American Indian Literatures and Cultures*. Ed. Elizabeth Hoffman Nelson. New York: Peter Lang, 2001. 93–108.

Gish, Robert F. "Word Medicine: Storytelling and Magic Realism in James Welch's *Fools Crow*." *AIQ* 14 (Fall 1990): 349–50.

Lowe, Lisa. *Immigrant Acts: On Asian American Cultural Politics*. Durham, NC: Duke UP, 1996.

McFarland, Ron. "The End in James Welch's Novels." *AIQ* 17 (Summer 1993): 319–27.

Nelson, Christopher. *Ethnographic Criticism in Native American Fiction*. PhD diss., University of Illinois, 2002.

Scheckter, John. "Now that the (water) Buffalo's Gone, James Welch and the Intercultural Novel." *Entering the 90s: The North American Experience*. Ed. Thomas E. Schirer. Sault St. Marie: Lake Superior UP, 1991. 101–7.

Shanley, Kathryn. "The Cinematic Eye in James Welch's *Fools Crow*." *GRAAT* 14 (1996): 131–38.

Velie, Alan. "The Indian Historical Novel." *Genre* 25.4 (1992): 391–405.

Welch, James. *Fools Crow*. New York: Penguin Books, 1986.

"The Primitive Has Escaped Control"

Narrating the Nation in *The Heartsong of Charging Elk*

ANDREA OPITZ
University of Washington

In 1889 in Marseilles, France, one of the Oglala Lakota performing in Buffalo Bill's Wild West awakens in the hospital after falling from his horse, left behind by the show that has traveled on to Italy. Abandoned in a foreign country where no one speaks his language, the protagonist of James Welch's *The Heartsong of Charging Elk* has exited the "safe" containment of Buffalo Bill's history lesson—in which he was cast as "first citizen"—and with it has quite literally exited the narrative space of American national history and culture; the "primitive," as Stuart Hall so poignantly puts it, "has escaped control" (187). Charging Elk escapes from the hospital and wanders around Marseilles for several days, finally arriving at a site that he recognizes as the place where the Wild West show had performed. He crosses the roundabout, walks up a wide street, eager to reach the field where the show had been staged. However, he finds that

> There was nothing there. Not one tent, not one hawker's stand, not even a fire pit where the Indian village had stood. He walked over to the large trampled circle of earth where the portable arena had been set up. The ground had been raked smooth. There was not a hoofprint on it, not one sign that the Indians, the cowboys, the soldiers, the vaqueros, the Deadwood stage, the buffaloes and horses had acted out their various dramas on this circle of earth. (48)

Charging Elk's "reading" of the former performance site reveals no trace, seemingly, of the show ever having been in Marseille. In vain, he looks for any evidence of the fire pits or the enactment of the drama of western conquest. However, he discovers that the enactment of dreams and fantasies does not leave any retrievable trace, and while the show was a real experience for him and the other performers who had cooked on those fire pits, the performance is only representative of something fabricated. Even though at first glance "there was nothing there," Charging Elk remembers what had been there and reveals the presence of an absence. Competing against the powerful forces of a cultural narrative that enacts what will soon become the dominant story of the West (and by extension the nation), he cannot recover the material and social histories and experiences that have been erased. Yet, he is able to witness and expose how every attempt has been made to "rake smooth" any trace left by these histories—traces that might disrupt the official narrative of the American nation and its conquest of the West.

Extending the decolonizing work he began with *Fools Crow* and continued with *Killing Custer*, Welch interrogates in his last novel the relation between U.S. government policies of removal, extinction, and assimilation and the ways in which cultural and national narratives—as produced, for example, by the traveling Wild West show—work to "naturalize" how Indigenous peoples imagine themselves in relation to these narratives. The Wild West show as popular cultural production creates "the Indian," literally removing Native Americans into the American (and European) imagination as "first citizens" of the nation, securely conquered within and tied to this nation's creation myth. Although he was part of the enactment, by being left behind Charging Elk ends up not moving into the Euramerican imagination. Left behind like a ghost in this highly ambiguous space, Charging Elk exposes how the "Indian" is repeatedly produced as vanishing, quite literally, at the end of the show. Quite contrary to the narrative of the "vanishing Indian," *Heartsong* conceptualizes cultural identity as *becoming*—an identity that is performed and conceived in relation to the fragmented memories and histories of his own culture, the representations of him as "exotic" and little more than a feathered creature, and legal and political regulations.

It is tempting to read Charging Elk's being stranded in France, his sense of alienation and racialized otherness, as an allegory for the forced removal of Native peoples onto reservations. Imagining the Lakotas' removal onto the Pine Ridge Reservation in the novel's prologue suggests as much. Yet, I suggest that the prologue functions more as a haunting reminder of the silenced and "naturalized" violence that informs the history of the West and of the nation. Charging Elk's remembering threatens to reintroduce into the narrative of the nation the history of racial violence, as well as the forgotten socialities of his people. What emerges in this site of radical displacement is a space in excess of the nation and yet painfully tied to it, a space in which the American Indian articulates the uncanny relocation of self in conflict with the American nation. Displacing national myths, Welch interrogates the (im)possibilities of Native American subjectivity within a national context by theorizing cultural and racialized identity as articulated and performed *in relation*, not *in essence*.

It is significant to note that Charging Elk's strange story is revealed through a narrative that more or less reads like a classic European bildungsroman. The genre's conventions, which narrate the maturing progress of a young individual who is to be reconciled with society, carry with them the possibility of allowing Welch to map his protagonist's complicated "merging" into the French social order. The bildungsroman functions to align the reader with the point of view of the protagonist, and Welch uses the reader's identification with Charging Elk's perspective throughout in order to highlight his displacement and alienation from his environment. For example, when Charging Elk is in prison, the novel works to displace the reader's identification, creating a sense of disorientation similar to what he himself experiences then and later during his first few months living with the Soulas family. Welch also critically links this conceptual displacement with larger issues of government policies concerning Indian education and assimilation policies. While he is still "on the loose" in the city, Charging Elk recalls an early childhood experience at the boarding school he attended for a year. The teacher pointed to him as she explained the word "Indian":

> He had sat in one of the rows of long tables watching the freckle-faced white woman write her words in white chalk on the black board: Boy. Girl. Cat. Dog. Fish. She showed them colored pictures of these creatures. The humans were pink, the cat yellow, and the dog black-and-white. The fish were orange and fat, unlike any he had ever seen. . . .
>
> He remembered the word "Indian." She had pointed directly at him, then at the board, and said "Indian." She made all the children say "Indian." Then she showed them a picture of a man they could not recognize. He had sharp toes, big thighs, and narrow shoulders; he wore a crown of blue and green and yellow feathers and an animal skin with dark spots. His eyes were large and round; his lips tiny and pursed. The white woman said "Indian." (56)

The shocking conceptual gap that Charging Elk experiences between the feathered "creature" and himself also becomes an alienating experience for the reader. What is constructed here is the figure of prehistoric and fantastic "Indianness": the racist fantasy that needs to project the "Indian" as artifact, as fetish, and as other. The production of the "Indian" and "savage" as artifact is made visible and located within the colonizing system rather than experienced as "natural" or "inherent" to the object himself. Yet, the teacher's move to identify Charging Elk with the sign of a feathered creature also works to override any other sense he may still have of himself. The scene works to align the reader with Charging Elk's alienation and to recognize the (il)logic on which the construction of him as a fixed sign of "exotic" otherness relies. The fantasy operates on three assumptions: that this "Indian" is a stable object of representation, that he is in some strange way identical with the sign, and that he identifies himself with it. This scene exposes how the government system—here supported by education—works to make American Indians internalize cultural, social, and racial hierarchies. To the class the figure is already that which they are not—a sign of seemingly stable representation of difference contained. The lesson of the Indian is not merely meant to teach the other children what creature the Indian is; by identifying Charging Elk with this picture, the teacher means to suggest that he is this—and nothing else—unless he assimilates and relinquishes the particularity of his experience and cultural identity. He would have to dis-identify himself from this sign, recognizing the creature as that which is him but from which he needs to "other" himself. Relinquishing his particularity in order to (try and) assimilate into a more civilized "image" operates within the same type of socializing that narrative bildungsroman conventions prescribe. The classroom is identified as an alien, and alienating, social order and thus offers an interesting counterpoint to the estrangement Charging Elk experiences trying to establish a life in Marseille.

Further, the image in the classroom is one example of how the racializing mechanism of assimilation confounds the logic by which the paradoxical relationship of Native Americans to the cultural terrain, as part of it and yet excluded from it, operates. American cultural narratives imagine the Indian as "first" or "original" citizen in order to deny the nation's historical emergence out of colonial conquest. What has to be concealed when American Indians are imagined as constituting part of the (white) American national narrative is that Natives first had to be wiped out, or at least brought to the brink of "vanishing," for this narrative to work. This idea of outward justification for domestic genocide is particularly interesting in light of the kind of history "lesson" with which Buffalo Bill traveled Europe. Displacing the racialized other as part of the nation's past—as the first figure of difference from which the nation emerges—the Wild West show plays its part in the drama in which the modernist narrative of the nation relies on cultural practices and productions to imagine the "Indian" as the country's "first citizen," whose perceived primitivism allows the nation's "civilization" to emerge as a chronological development. In this context Welch stages the show as representative of the ways in which cultural narratives are complicit in the workings of American national narratives, repeatedly performing the "Indian" as essential to its imaginative project and yet paradoxically excluded from it. Buffalo Bill's Wild West traveled through Europe promoting Cody's version of the history of the American West as a "clean, dramatic, and compelling narrative [that] made the conquest of savages central" (White 11).

Richard White argues that Cody inverted the history of the West by casting the Indians as aggressors, constantly attacking white settlers. Furthermore, by staging famous and not so famous battles and so-called Indian races, the Wild West show pronounced itself on posters and programs as a "full and complete history" enacting "vivid and realistic scenes from the Pioneer History of America." Yet, even though Buffalo Bill's Wild West means to be a history lesson, its "exhibit" of life in the West is divorced from the diverse histories that emerge in the West. In the novel, this becomes apparent when the French audiences show themselves as so enraptured by the spectacle that they are unable to distinguish performance from real life. After the shows were over, Charging Elk remembers, audience members would enter "family lodges, as though the mother fixing dinner or the sleeping child in its cradleboard were part of the entertainment" (51). The way history is presented and perceived by the audiences merges entertainment with the after-show activities of the performers so that even their everyday activities become nothing more than products of a culture "long gone," displaced into the past. One of the characters in the novel recalls that in Buffalo Bill's narrative the Natives are "disappearing—like the bison" (137). In fact, Buffalo Bill tells the audience that "their culture is dying and soon they will be gone too," as if there is no reasonable cause for this disappearing act. The paradox lies in the fact that while the rhetoric of "first citizen" merges the American Indian with the nation-building story, Indigenous peoples are cast as different—so different that they cannot be imagined as part of a progressive nation unless they "assimilate." Especially as Buffalo Bill's show travels through Europe, the complicated relationship between historiography and narrative cannot be understood merely in its western setting but has to be read in the context of the U.S. nation, because the show produces American national identity in relation to the history of the West.

The paradoxical cultural and national imaginings within which Charging Elk is caught and his complicated relationship to the legal discourses that prevent him from returning home place another character into a highly ambivalent relationship to interrelated workings of legal, political, and representational discourses. Vice-consul Bell, diplomatic representative for the Indian performers, functions in this novel as representative of official cultural and political national discourse. In his often frustrated situation of having to deal with the bureaucratic complications that ensue due to Charging Elk's complicated status in relation to the United States and the mispronouncement of the young Lakota's death, Bell finds himself in active dialogue with what it means to be "American," with who gets to pronounce national belonging, and with the continued violence of pronouncing someone dead who is very much alive.

Bell is torn between official discourse, cultural narratives, and the actual presence of an Indian, which he cannot himself erase. The first complication of Charging Elk's status erupts when the French officials suggest that he entered the country illegally: "he is not a citizen of the United States, he does not hold a valid passport" (114). This legal fact collides with the cultural narrative that has been traveling across Europe as America's representative. René Soulas tries to correct the officials: "But the law is misguided in this case, *capitaine*. The Peau-Rouge is clearly a citizen of America. He is the original citizen. Buffalo Bill said so" (114). Even the captain has to confess that he finds this fact confusing; he assumed that Buffalo Bill's assertions during the show were true and only now finds out that the U.S. government claims that the "*indiens* were not real citizens of their own country" (115). The already paradoxical situation turns into a farce when Charging Elk is declared dead (in error) by the hospital officials, and Bell finds himself fighting to correct this mistake, while he himself at times thinks of Charging Elk (and his people) as barely alive. When Bell first visited Charging Elk in his cell he could not help but reflect on the Indian as being of a "strange race of people [who were] still attempting to live in the past with their feathers and beads" (82). Even though it occurs to him that Charging Elk is not an American citizen, he still pronounces him a citizen because of a special agreement with the Wild West show under which the performers are entitled to diplomatic representation. In a way framing his "ward" within a national context gives Bell more leverage, while he himself—off duty, on the way home—finds himself resorting to the generalizing "assimilate or die" narrative. Bell's initial attempts to write off Charging Elk in order not to assume responsibility remain futile, and thus he has to acknowledge not only his responsibility for Charging Elk but also the young Lakota's persisting presence despite his bureaucratic erasure. Bell becomes increasingly frustrated with the French government's handling of Charging Elk's case, and when the official statements claim that there was "no indien in the Préfecture on Christmas Eve," he is confronted with the fact that in his stewardship Charging Elk has vanished (179). The Indian has become "nonexistent, a ghost you might say" (178)—a narrative twist that makes the French official story sound very much like the U.S. narrative. Instead of an anachronism in the present or a dead Indian, Bell comes to realize that in Charging Elk, he and René Soulas "still have a very real *indien* on our hands" (179).

Welch's interrogations into the ways in which American Indians are constructed as a necessary, and yet excluded, part of the U.S. nation and its historical and cultural narratives offer insightful parallels to the model of cultural critique developed by Lisa Lowe in her study of Asian American cultural politics, *Immigrant Acts*. Cultural productions and historical narratives as spaces that have to be continuously interrogated and theorized, Lowe argues, "because culture is the contemporary repository of memory, of history[;] it is through culture, rather than government, that alternative forms of subjectivity, collectivity, and public life are imagined" (22). A cultural critique such as this considers the different, particular histories of Indigenous, immigrant, migrant, and diasporic experiences in the United States as a way to reimagine the relations among various groups and to the "dominant" culture so that the national cultural terrain can be questioned and reshaped.

In this novel Welch redirects conventional notions of home, culture, and belonging into a critique of radical displacement policies, which even today leave Native Americans disenfranchised in a segregated place, because remembering and enacting the "first citizen" and forgetting the violence done against them are still an intricate part of American national narratives. As part of the national cultural terrain American Indian literatures and cultures occupy a crucial space that should be read and studied as continuously *challenging* the ways U.S. national culture fixes "otherness" in contained, "marginal" places, as *interrogating* the way U.S. cultural productions narrate the nation's histories, and as *remembering* the particularities of diverse American Indian histories and cultural practices through histories of violence and displacement. This cultural critique works to create spaces for counterdiscourse from which new forms of subjectivity emerge that contest the models of subject formation on which the nation relies.

WORKS CITED

Hall, Stuart. "The Local and the Global: Globalization and Ethnicity." *Dangerous Liaisons: Gender, Nation, and Postcolonial Perspectives*. Ed. Anne McClintock, Anmir Mufti, and Ella Shohat. Minneapolis: U of Minnesota P, 1997. 173–87.

Lowe, Lisa. *Immigrant Acts: On Asian American Cultural Politics*. Durham: Duke UP, 1996.

Welch, James. *The Heartsong of Charging Elk*. New York: Anchor Books, 2001.

White, Richard. "Frederick Jackson Turner and Buffalo Bill." *The Frontier in American Culture*. Ed. James R. Grossman. Berkeley: U of California P, 1994. 6–65.